The Real You Is Immortal:

Dear Joseph,

Happy Birthday

With lots of Love,

Mom

May 11, 2016

The Real You Is Immortal:

Whether You Like It or Not!

WILLIAM F. PILLOW JR.

ISBN: 1517702232
ISBN 13: 9781517702236
Library of Congress Control Number: 2015917196
CreateSpace Independent Publishing Platform
North Charleston, South Carolina

Also by William Pillow:

Love and Immortality: Long Journey of My Heart
Meet Yourself Again for the First Time
Mind, Body, & Spirit: Challenges of Science and Faith
Spirituality Beyond Science and Religion
Souls Are Real! Death Is Not!

Acknowledgments

Our Creator, my birth family, and our married family naturally come first for my gratitude in being able to write this book. I especially express my love, respect, and appreciation for my beloved wife, Betty, whose soul has passed into Heaven. I give special thanks to our son, Brad, and to our daughter, Val, for their loving personal support and encouragement for my writing.

I especially appreciate their tolerance for the subjects and contents of my books. So please do *not* blame them for whatever you disagree with in my writing.

I am indebted, as are we all, to the survivors of sudden cardiac arrest who reported on their near-death experiences. Without their fearless testimonies and the progress of dedicated researchers, the rest of us would still fear death and be wondering about the place that religions call "Heaven."

I am particularly grateful to those researchers and academicians who were willing to risk their personal standing among peers and colleagues by breaking through the glass walls that enclose and restrain science and scientists from contemplating and exploring what is sometimes called the "spiritual" world, beyond the "material" reality.

Introduction

"The most beautiful experience is to meet the mysterious.
This is the source of all art and scholarly pursuit.
He who has never had this experience, is not capable
of rapture, and cannot stand motionless with amazement,
is as good as dead. His eyes are closed."

ALBERT EINSTEIN

You have never read another book like this one! And I never could have imagined everything I found about life and death that you will read here! Basically, this book documents how I changed from a traditional Southern Baptist Christian and a devoted skeptic of the paranormal, during my anxious search for answers to my growing fear of losing my beloved wife, Betty, to death.

Obviously this book's title is radical. But it is supported by many scientific, medical, and psychological revelations that now are either acknowledged or are felt likely to be true. So this book may read like science fiction—but it is *nonfiction*! Why? Because this book discusses natural "phenomena," which the Oxford Dictionary defines as "facts or situations that are observed to exist or happen, especially ones whose cause or explanation is in question." Therefore you will be introduced to *experiential* evidence—based on *perceptible* human experiences—with which you likely are *not* familiar, whose *causes* are "in question."

For example, four unrelated teenage boys *each* tried to commit suicide five times, once a year at his chosen time of year. Later, each mother admitted having attempted an abortion at *that* particular time of year. Yet the boys' fetal brains were too *immature* to have "known" and "remembered" that! This book therefore will challenge your thinking *how* these natural phenomena could result from previously unknown "causes" that were *both* imperceptible and inexplicable.

Because these phenomena involve physical and mental early human development, you will want to assess the credibility of these "causes," based upon experiential evidence of their impacts in pediatrics, psychology, neurobiology, neuroscience, and other research disciplines.

The primary focus obviously is on substantiating the title claim, so far as that *seems* humanly possible. Yet the very nature of this book reaches far beyond anything you might even imagine, just like its title. So please let me suggest how *I as a reader* would approach this book, "If *any* of this could *possibly* be true, does that hold any conceivable meaning for my loved ones or for me?"

But this book's contents also apply to two current issues that continue to fuel this world's increasing malevolence. One is the brash *willingness* by terrorists to *seek* death for *false promises* of reward in Heaven. The other are the now *documented* causes of rash acts by young people whose *very early* lives left them feeling *marginalized* in life. For these two causes, I do ask your serious consideration.

Obviously, these two additional claims may seem almost as radical as the book's title. That is why this book is *unlike* any other you ever have read! So *please* try to suppress your likely shock or anger at discussions that seem to conflict with your cherished beliefs—at least until you read how beliefs suppress continued brain growth.

Nevertheless, as the author I willingly accept responsibility for everything that this book contains. Only after you finish the book, however, will it be possible for you to fathom what these diverse findings might actually mean for you, your loved ones, *and* humankind. Much of the book will be *unimaginable*, even *controversial*, to many people. Some readers will even accuse me of disrupting their comfortable beliefs and life styles. But, as you may have heard it asked, "Please don't kill the messenger!"

I did *not* write this book to *judge* whether your beliefs are right or wrong! I wrote it *only* to share with you what I found to be life changing for me. Even as often as I seriously questioned my sanity in publishing this book, my concerns about the state of our world still urged me to do so! So remember Ben Franklin's famous saying, "Nothing ventured; nothing gained?"

Realizing that you may want to verify or expand on what you read here, I have included a very extensive bibliography in the back of the book. Please use it! Many of the references are available online.

One

RELIGION

"Now I lay me down to sleep.
I pray the Lord my soul to keep.
If I should die before I wake,
I pray the Lord my soul to take."

THE NEW ENGLAND PRIMER, 1683

Religion has been a part of my entire life, so it continues to be a central part of my quest for answers. I learned this prayer in Sunday school at the First Baptist Church in Farmville, Virginia and it became my bedtime ritual. A comfortable Southern Baptist faith remained with me until 1998. That year and the next decade eventually led me to what you will find in this book, during my still-continuing quest for answers that seem to evade us in ordinary life. But, in case you skipped the Introduction, I will repeat, "I did *not* write this book to *judge* whether your beliefs are right or wrong! I wrote it *only* to share with you what I found to be life changing for me."

As we became a family, however, my military service and work took us to different parts of the United States. After we permanently settled in Indianapolis, Indiana, we became Northern Baptists, then Presbyterians, and most recently Methodists. I served as deacon, elder, and trustee at the Northminster Presbyterian Church, in Indianapolis.

I remember *that* 1998 very well. While my wife, Betty, was in a senior citizens' class about art—her favorite subject—in a Block's store in Indianapolis, I spent the time there in the Washington Square Mall's bookstore. Although soon noticing a book on the front "sale" display with an intriguing title, I scanned other shelves for books that might be worth buying. Not finding any and with Betty's class almost over, I bought that first one with the fascinating title, *just for laughs*. I still was a devout skeptic about the paranormal, a lifelong trait. That book was Carol Bowman's *Children's Past Lives: How Past Life Memories Affect Your Child.*

In a sense the rest is history, from 1998 on. I didn't read Bowman's book for a *very* long time, its title soon forgotten. But I credit it, once I *did* read it, as the beginning of my search for answers. That quest began with my realization that death would steal my beloved wife, Betty, from me after 57 years of a wonderful life together. That year, Betty was found to have breast cancer. I soon learned that I had prostate cancer and later thyroid cancer. Meanwhile, Betty had a stroke that left her bed and wheelchair dependent, so I personally cared for her at home—I had retired five years earlier.

Yet mortal death had never bothered me earlier in life. Despite eventually having accommodated to death through occasional funerals of friends, one haunting childhood memory remained with me. It involved my grandfather's burial. I had nightmares about it afterwards, thinking, "How could Grandpa ever dig through all that dirt to reappear in Heaven." However, that seems to reflect the unquestioned acceptance I continued to have about Christian teachings—until some time after 1998.

In the five years before Betty passed over in 2009, I had changed from a traditional Southern Baptist Christian and a devoted skeptic of the paranormal, during my anxious search for answers to my growing fear of losing my beloved wife, Betty, to death.

Religion and Death

From the memory of my Grandfather's burial and the untimely death of a high school classmate in an auto accident—all the way to 1998—I never spent any time considering what death *really* represents. Naturally I had heard a lot about Heaven, but not very detailed. So I really had not worried about reuniting with Betty there.

But when I first began to agonize about death separating us, I started wondering if anyone else had the answer or was even as concerned as I was. Of course, then as it is now, death is a subject everyone *avoids* mentioning—except when someone you know dies. Then and now, funerals naturally flood the eyes with memories of the *past*, instead of at least *hinting* at the *promises* of the afterlife.

So I thought maybe I could learn more by digging into religion's past. That seemed the logical place to start, since preachers are the ones in charge of death, so to speak. Of course, Christianity talks about death, but any reunion it mentions with loved ones seemed far distant in the future.

Naturally, you would expect the ministers in our church to ask me, "Why didn't you let your Christian faith help you?" As a pharmacist, of course, I was very familiar with tranquilizers and antidepressants. But to me, Christianity was a belief. So I checked the dictionary, which said "faith" is "complete trust or confidence in someone or something rather than proof." That made me even more curious. So I *really* dug back in time, much farther than you might even imagine!

After the Last Ice Age

Down through time, our ancestors seem to have sensed hidden truths as they buried their loved ones. They sustained a hope that has forever dwelt in the mind of man. At its heart, our forefathers instinctively believed in a Supreme Power. But you may be surprised just *how* long ago mankind acknowledged that unseen forces do exist—and they even symbolized their beliefs and fears through some sort of structure and worship.

Until the last ice age loosed its grip about 9,600 BCE—that was *almost twelve thousand years* ago—our ancestors were largely hunters and gatherers who still lived in hut settlements of a few hundred people. But something happened around that time, which *National Geographic* magazine's cover story called "The Birth of Religion," in an article by Charles Mann. That cover also claimed "The World's First Temple." However, the term "religion" would not be *needed* for another almost *ten thousand years*.

Confucius, Buddha, Socrates, Aristotle, Jesus, and Mohammed would not have been born until about *ten millenia* later. In the context of time, the Great Pyramid of Giza and Stonehenge had not been built for another *seven* thousand years. The invention of writing about five thousand years ago (i.e., 3200 BCE) in the Near East helped chronicle the history of "religion." The Pyramid Texts from ancient Egypt are one of the oldest known "religious" inscriptions, dating over four thousand years ago (i.e., 2300 BCE). The Dead Sea Scrolls originated around two thousand years later.

The remainder of this chapter therefore offers details I gleaned from many online and print sources. You therefore may draw your own personal conclusions. Mine are shaped around learning how variegated early religion was and the extent of human factors involved.

Some readers may consider this chapter biased or inaccurate. I therefore crosschecked different sources for each section, many from authenticated early Christian history. You can access full references in the Bibliography.

Early Religions

I found it fascinating—the computer offers a treasure trove of information. For example, I was surprised how little I knew about the time Jesus lived and how reports about His life and crucifixion were spread to Gentile (i.e., non-Jewish) people. To my great surprise, I also discovered how the bible I grew up with had, in a sense, "evolved," as had religions. So, because the central theme of my book naturally will impinge upon religion, I will include more detail about these human institutions than you may feel is necessary. However, you may be surprised by what you find here.

Early Christianity

Judaism as a religion first appears in Greek records more than a thousand years BCE (i.e., BC). Scholars estimate Jesus' birth to be around 4 BCE and His crucifixion about 30-33 CE (i.e., AD). He and His followers were Jewish. The latter therefore were Jewish converts. Christianity did not become primarily Gentile (i.e., non-Jewish) until the early to mid-second century.

In the late first century CE, there was a document called the *Jewish-Christian Didache,* which is said to best reflect the Jewish-Jesus movement (i.e., "The Way"). It focused on Mosaic Law and the love of God and neighbor, and described the observance of Jewish traditions alongside baptism and recitation of the Lord's Prayer. Solomon Schechter and Kaufmann Kohler offered an online discussion of the Didache.

Apparently His followers' view of Jesus at that time was as a "charismatic prophet." Jews eventually disavowed Him as their long-awaited messiah. Since Mark's Gospel, the first one to appear, was written in Greek, he translated the Hebrew term "messiah" into "christos" (i.e., "anointed one" in Greek), which later became, in English, "Jesus [the] Christ."

It was in John's Gospel, and only in that Gospel, that Jesus proclaims His divine identity, speaking in what New Testament scholars call the "I am" sayings. Yet the Apostle Paul was the first person to claim Jesus' divinity. His writings started around 51 CE, some twenty years after Jesus' crucifixion, but before John's Gospel appeared about 85-90 CE.

Beginning around the middle of the first century, the Apostle Paul's epistles were responsible for recruiting Gentile believers from across the Roman Empire. People were finding their way into Jewish synagogues and many Gentiles were deciding to convert. Nevertheless, this attraction of Gentiles to Jewish Christianity was large enough that the Jewish authorities had to develop a program for the incorporation of new converts *into Judaism.*

The idea that "Jesus died for my sins" first entered the Christian tradition in the same epistle in which Jesus was called the "new Passover lamb." It was Paul, writing to the Corinthians about the year 54 CE, who first used these words: "Jesus died for our sins in accordance with the scriptures."

Paul seems to have imported this from his Jewish background and thorough familiarity with the Old Testament, and extrapolated it from the Jewish Day of Atonement (i.e., Yom Kippur). Paul (i.e., Saul of Tarsus) was a few years younger than Jesus and changed his name and life after his experience on the Damascus road. That event seems to have happened several years after Jesus' crucifixion.

Moreover, Paul was born to Jewish parents who had Roman citizenship. He acknowledges that he had lived as a Pharisee, the strictest sect of Judaism. He had continued to persecute the more liberal Hellenist believers in the Way and bring them to the Jerusalem council for punishment and sometimes death.

Yet the term "original sin" is unknown in the Jewish Scriptures. Therefore, the Christian Church's teachings on this doctrine were antithetical to the core principles of the Jewish Torah and its prophets. Jesus' followers all knew this. Therefore "original sin" played no role with them.

In Romans 5, Paul addresses the matter of sin. In verse 12 he says, "Therefore . . . sin came into the world through one man, and death came through sin, and so death spread to all because all have sinned" (NRSV). Later in that chapter, Paul juxtaposes the sin of Adam with the righteousness of Christ: "Just as by the one man's disobedience the many were made sinners, so by the one man's obedience the many will be made righteous."

In contrast to his fellow theologians, Augustine reaffirmed this in 396-430 CE and made it "inherited" sin through his slight mistranslation of the Greek in Paul's letters—meaning that sin was passed biologically from Adam to all his descendants. Thus it became a cornerstone to Christianity, despite modern scholars' view that Paul would have rejected Augustine's idea of biological transmission. Of course, in Genesis, God simply sentenced Adam to till the ground for food and eventually die. Peter Nathan authored "The Original View of Original Sin."

But Paul's emphasis on Jesus' divinity could not have come from Jesus' storied virgin birth because his letters never mention such a miraculous birth or either Mary or Joseph. Neither could Jesus' miracles have been responsible, since more than fifty miracles by earlier prophets are included in the Old Testament.

Paul's letters never described his experience on the road to Damascus, which seems to account for his conversion to Christianity. However, in his Second Letter to the Corinthians, 12:1-6 he tells this story:

"I know a man in Christ who fourteen years ago who was caught up to the third Heaven—whether in the body or out of the body I do not know, God knows. And I know that this man was caught up into paradise ... and he heard things that cannot be told, which man may not utter."

Later you can compare what just may be Paul's Damascus Road vision—which happened about fourteen years before his Epistles began—with experiences described by near-death survivors today. Emperor Nero martyred Paul in Rome about 67 CE. A booklet about the Apostle Paul is available online, "Jewish Law and Early Christianity."

Influence of Rome

Thereafter, for almost three centuries, Christianity experienced turbulent times. Remember that its spread by then had encompassed the entire Roman Empire. It was characterized by inner conflicts from all sides, some of those perhaps reminiscent of Paul's different exhortations to various groups. Obviously there were upheavals, too, during the flux of Rome's politics, social customs, and economy.

Doctrinal debates raged, working through scriptural interpretations and understanding. Development of the New Testament canon was not done until the early fourth century CE. The Gospel of Mark was the first written, near 60 CE in Greek. Matthew dates to about mid-60s CE. Luke wrote his gospel and Acts around 65 CE. John appeared close to 85-90 CE. But not until the discoveries at Nag Hammadi in 1945, was it evident that fifty or more other Christian manuscripts also had been circulating during Christianity's early years.

The third century was a time of intense anarchy. Civil wars, barbarian invasions, and plague wracked the Roman Empire. Widespread troubles left pagan worshippers feeling abandoned by their gods. Christianity seemed more attractive.

But persecution of Christians increased. Romans started blaming Christians, whose earlier refusal to pay homage to the emperor and to state gods had previously been overlooked by Rome in peaceful and prosperous times. Professor Harold Attridge and other religious authorities prepared an extensive online discussion on "The Diversity of Early Christianity."

The "Constantine" Effect

But in the third and fourth centuries, a large part of the church did not yet believe that Jesus was divine. Some even wondered if the Holy Spirit was another God. Arius, a very gifted elder in Alexandria, was the leading spokesman for those who did not believe Jesus was divine. Athanasius, then a very influential assistant to the bishop of Alexandria, was the leader for the opposite view that Jesus was divine in the same way as God the Father:

> "Athanasius's main disagreement with Arius concerned salvation: we are saved because in Christ God Himself became a human being and died a human death. God became a human to make humans divine; the immortal became mortal to raise mortals to immortality." From: "#108: Athanasius on Christ."

Proponents of each view (Arius vs Athanasius) created dissention among the churches. So, at the 325 CE Council of Nicaea called by the Roman Emperor Constantine, he permitted Christianity to become an acceptable Roman religion as were the Pagans. This legitimized the first institutional Christianity in the Roman Catholic Church. But Constantine wanted a consensus declaration that Roman converts would be required to believe. Most of the 360 bishops in attendance agreed on the Trinity and the Nicene Creed, some of whom later expressed their reluctance in private. This was amended and ratified at the First Council at Constantinople in 381 CE.

Yet, Athanasius became bishop of Alexandria upon the death of Alexander in 328 CE. In Athanasius' 39th Festal Letter in 367 CE, he named the twenty-seven books to become the New Testament. He also named seven other books "which have been appointed by the Fathers as reading matter for those who have just come forward and which to be instructed in the doctrine of piety." Athanasius also wrote, "yet mention is nowhere made of the apocrypha; rather they are a fabrication of the heretics ..." So the Roman Catholic Church did not officially canonize the Apocrypha until the Council of Trent in 1545 CE.

The term "apocrypha" means "hidden things" in Greek. New Testament apocrypha includes twenty-seven other documents that were considered "early Christian writings." Old Testament apocrypha includes twenty-nine early Jewish writings. Further information is available online.

After Constantine's death in 337 CE, the forcible expansion of Christianity on the Roman populace led to some resentment. Succeeding Constantine's three sons, Julian the Apostate tried in vain to stem the tide of Christianity. Paganism had still been a permitted part of the culture.

A generation later, Theodosius and his western counterpart, Gracian, recognized Christianity as the official religion of the Roman Empire in 380 CE. Severe punishment was enforced for Paganism and especially "heretic" Arianism. After four hundred years, at the beginning of the fifth century, Christianity had grown from a fledgling mystery cult into the Roman Catholic Church, which was on nearly equal terms with the Roman Emperor himself. This was discussed online in "Christianity: The Official Religion of the Roman Empire."

Secret Gospel of Thomas

Among the fifty or more Christian manuscripts discovered at Nag Hammadi in 1945, one has drawn a lot of attention and seems worth examining separately. It is one of the Christian Apocrypha called the *Secret Gospel of Thomas*. The disciple may not have written it entirely by himself, since he was martyred in 72 CE in India. However, the *Gospel of Thomas* contained Jesus' private sayings to him, of which John was aware.

In his gospel, John voiced disagreement with Thomas about those teachings, apparently by portraying him as "Doubting Thomas" who "needed to see the spear marks in Jesus' side before believing." But Mark, Matthew, and Luke mention Thomas only as one of "the twelve." Moreover, Christian scholars feel that many of John's Christian contemporaries revered Thomas as an extraordinary apostle, entrusted with Jesus' "secret words."

However, it is also worth noting that the Gospels of John and Thomas also contain some similar teachings. Yet Thomas takes Jesus' private teachings in a different direction from John. For example, the "divine light that Jesus represents" is shared by all humanity, since we all are made in the image of God. Therein, the Gospel of Thomas initiates a central theme of Jewish, and eventually Christian, mysticism a thousand years later—the "image of God" is hidden in everyone, typically without his or her awareness, but secretly linking God and all humanity. Thomas' Jesus seems to reaffirm this in His other private teachings, like the following:

> "Since you are my twin and my true companion, examine yourself and learn who you are ... since you will be called my [twin], ... although you do not understand it yet ... you will be called 'the one who knows himself.' For whosoever has not known himself knows nothing, but whosoever has known himself has simultaneously come to know the depth of all things."

Jesus is said to have taken Thomas into the wilderness to tell him those "secret words." When Thomas was later asked what Jesus had told him, he reputedly refused, believing that his companions would stone him to death for blasphemy.

Jesus is said to have given Thomas a special assignment to go to India. A parallel accounting suggests that Jesus, as an Essene, had Himself spent time in India. He was said to be in training with yoga and spiritual masters there during the so-called "silent" period before His publicized ministry began. So Thomas developed a following in India. Records and relics apparently exist there attesting to his revered presence. Hinduism believes in the soul and in reincarnation.

Excerpts about the Secret Gospel of Thomas are from *Beyond Belief: The Secret Gospel of Thomas* by Elaine Pagels.

Development of the Bible

The Judeo/Christian Bible is often called "the word of God" or "the inspired word of God." Millions of people read this bible in a variety of languages today. For centuries, humans have made interpretations from early manuscript languages and within individual languages. Original languages in which early Jewish and Christian manuscripts appeared were Aramaic (common at Jesus' time), Hebrew, Greek (common during Roman occupation), and Latin (preferred by the Catholic Church). Perhaps it is no surprise therefore, that no bible sold anytime in the past several centuries can be considered an exact reproduction of the earliest Jewish or Christian manuscripts existing when Christianity was being formed among Jewish followers in the first century CE. Of course, translations are the work of many people, not just a single individual. Translators sometimes attempted to interpret earlier versions for a variety of reasons, some not necessarily to provide the most theologically accurate meaning of the original. Moreover, meaning often cannot be captured accurately between different languages. These claims are not intended as heresy but as actuality that illuminate the Judeo/Christian Bible as spiritual encouragement rather than literal history. Here is a chronology of different versions of the bible:

Earliest Hebrew language Old Testament, about First Century = Dead Sea Scrolls

Earliest New Testament = Codex Sinaiticus handwritten in Greek around 350-70 CE.

180	Old Latin or *Italia* version Old Testament, in South and North Africa
367	New Testament canon of 27 books in 39th Festal Letter of Athanasius
405	Latin Vulgate (Official Vatican) developed from Old Latin by Jerome First bible to mention "cross" (from Latin "crux")
1380	John Wycliff's translation of Old Latin into English; asst. John Purvey further edited (after poisoning him) to conform to Jerome's version
1516	Erasmus' "Greek-Latin Parallel of New Testament" (not from Vulgate)
1525	Tyndale's first printing of New Testament in English translated from Erasmus's "Greek-Latin Parallel of New Testament," Luther's German version, and the Vulgate

1535   Myles Coverdale finished translating the Old Testament and printed the first complete English bible (carrying on Tyndale's work)

1537   John Rogers printed second complete English bible, but the first translated from the original biblical Hebrew and Greek

1539   At bequest of King Henry VIII, Thomas Cranmer, Archbishop of Canterbury, hired Myles Coverdale to publish the first legal English "Great Bible" (commonly known as Matthew-Tyndale Bible)

1560   The complete "Geneva Bible" was published ("Breeches Bible" for clothing God fashioned for Adam and Eve after their expulsion), the first bible to add numbered verses to chapters and marginal notes and references, retaining over 90% of Tyndale's original translation

1568   Revision of the "Great Bible" known as the "Bishop's Bible"

1611   Release of King James Bible to replace the "Bishop's Bible," to result from work of fifty scholars, but with scriptural references only for word clarification or cross-references

1777   First publication of King James New Testament in America

1782   First publication of King James Bible in America

1844   Codex Sinaiticus found - earliest complete copy of New Testament, from fourth century, handwritten in vernacular Greek, with Old Testament written in Septuagint, version of Greek adopted by early Greek-speaking Christians

Development of Christian Religions
Judaism   1,000   (BCE)

Roman Catholic   325   (CE) (Recognized by Roman Emperor Constantine)

1517   Protestant Reformation (revolt against Roman Catholic Church), with the formation of different Protestant denominations, differing on key points of doctrine

1534   King Henry VIII's "Act of Supremacy" created (Anglican) Church of England declaring himself the head of the Anglican Church of England

1550   Effort to Protestantize the Anglican Church but lasted only 112 years

1553   Beginning of five-year reign of Mary Tudor ("Bloody Mary"), who wanted to return England to the Roman Catholic Church and burned Rogers, Cranmer, and many other "reformers" at the stake

Timeline of Christian History

For readers who are interested, an online "Timeline of Christian History" is available, stretching from Abraham to Pope Francis today. Some of the items in the two preceding date lists are included there too but some are not, since various references were used for the two date lists.

Abrahamic Heritage

Judaism, Christianity, and Islam share a common heritage: Abraham. Muhammad considered Abraham's first son, Ishmael, to be the ancestor of those people for whom Islam was developed. You may recall that Abraham's wife, Sarai, in aging, feared that she would never bear a male heir for Abraham. So she encouraged him to have Ishmael through Haggai, her handmaiden. Once Sarai had Isaac, however, she sent Haggai and Ishmael into the wilderness to grant Isaac first-born rights from Abraham. Apparently, Ishmael and his mother survived. In that common heritage with Judaism and Christianity, Muhammad acknowledged Abraham (i.e. Ibrahim) as a great prophet and patriarchal figure and adopted Judaism's monotheism (i.e., one God).

After Muhammad's visions from the angel Gabriel, beginning around 610 CE, the Qur'an eventually was developed. It was used, along with the hadith (i.e., traditions) and sharia (i.e., law) for Muslim conduct. Hovering over the application of sharia by jurists, however, has been the longstanding tradition of tribal patriarchy, wherein the head of the family retains indisputable rights over all family members. The concept of "shame" seems to prevail as defensible for most of the family head's decisions and actions.

Islam acknowledges Jesus as a great prophet but disavows His divinity and, therefore, the concept of the Trinity. Like Judaism and Christianity, Islam adopted a version of the "end-times." An online comparison is entitled "Christianity vs Islam."

Recall, too, the Catholic Church's rise to power in ancient Rome, almost equal to that of the emperors. In some ways this was a "theocracy," similar to the theocracy as the ultimate "governing" authority in some Muslim countries today.

From Reason to Faith

You may have heard that a chasm exists between science and religion. However that is not a recent occurrence. Actually, religious anthropologist Charles Freeman's book *The Closing of the Western Mind* shows how this began as early as the fifth century CE. Freeman says this culminated from the Apostle Paul's attack on Greek philosophy; Christian theologians' adoption of Platonism; and Roman emperors' enforcement of orthodoxy in their desperation to maintain order throughout the Empire. "The imposition of orthodoxy went hand in hand with a stifling of any form of independent reasoning. The struggle between religion and science had now entered a new phase."

Yet it was Thomas Aquinas, who apparently revived the Aristotelian approach to knowing things, beginning around 1250 CE, who seems to have laid the foundations for the scientific revolution.

Religion in the News

Today's news media seldom misses a day without an item about religion. Collectively, we watch, read, or hear diverse views from individuals and institutions about religion, slipping percentages in church membership or attendance, or social issues. The following represent a few of these.

On September 25, 2015, Fox News televised a one-hour special entitled "Losing Faith in America?" But it portrayed the loss of participation in recent decades among Christian churches in America and in Catholicism, *not* loss of faith in America itself. (http://www.foxnews.com/on-air/fox-news-reporting/2015/09/23/fox-news-reporting-losing-faith-america) That special report depicted the general trend, with some examples that have survived and a few that have grown. It also examined opinions why both are occurring as well as general observations by and about young peoples' and adults' views.

Recently, a very cogent analysis was offered of the reason that religion exists, as follows:

- "Religion is part of the human security system that serves to bank the fires of anxiety. This anxiety was born in the breakthrough from consciousness to self-consciousness in our evolutionary journey. It was that breakthrough that made human life as we know it possible. As self-conscious creatures, we embrace questions of meaning and finitude and thus we enter the state of chronic anxiety that marks all human life. Self-conscious human beings also embrace the reality of living in time. When we were merely conscious creatures, we were driven only by our biological needs. Conscious animals are born, eat, grow, reproduce, and die in endless cycles. They do not ask whether life has meaning. They do not anticipate or worry about dying. They do not embrace mortality or prepare for coming future events. So it is self-consciousness alone that creates in us human beings that state of chronic anxiety that is alone the hallmark of human life.
- "We human beings deal with this chronic anxiety in many ways. We use drugs. Animals do not do that. Human beings use caffeine as a stimulus to get us started each day and we use alcohol to slow us down. We use tranquilizers so extensively that we have created a billion dollar pharmaceutical industry to supply our demands. We use tobacco to recreate the security of nursing and we create religion to answer the questions of meaning and mortality.

- "[But] religion cannot serve this function if it is only "relatively true." Security demands that religion be made ultimately true with no doubts allowed. That is why the Pope has to be infallible. That is why the claim must be made for the Bible to be inerrant. That is why we assert that our religion is the only "true religion." It is out of these claims that the need arises for us to impose this "one true faith" on all people. The conversion mentality is simply part of that. In my opinion, this need for security is an aspect of retarded growth in what it means to be human, and the religion that it produces so often seeks to keep us in a state of childlike immaturity. Beyond this childlike quest for security, I believe we need to discover one other dimension of self-consciousness. It is the one that beckons us to grasp a new maturity. In this dimension of self-consciousness we do not need to be "born again," we rather need to grow up.

- "Maturity comes not in our constant pretending to be secure. It comes, rather, when we embrace the fact that it is human to be anxious and then to dare to embrace that reality. To live with integrity in a radically insecure world is, I believe, the meaning of the Christian life. As long as any religion, Christianity and Islam included, believes that it possesses the ultimate truth, it will traffic in security-giving tactics and panaceas.

- "When each religious system recognizes that ultimate truth is not something we possess, but something toward which we walk but never achieve in the human pilgrimage, then a new integrity will come to those traditional faith circles. The need to convert another to my "true religion" will cease. This conversion idea today repels more people than it attracts, a sure sign that it is dying. Whether a new stage of religious maturity will be born to take its place is not quite as clear. That, however, is where the future of Christianity lies."

The above was reproduced with their kind permission from Bishop John Shelby Spong's weekly publication, "A New Christianity for a New World."

Nevertheless, according to John Shelby Spong, there is a rise in evangelicalism among religions around the globe. Moreover, he says, there is a lingering of the "tribal" interpretation of the God of the Hebrew Old Testament, meaning that each religion considers itself the "chosen people." Different religions down through history therefore felt it was God's will for them to convert or destroy others—the "un-chosen people." This was from Spong's video presentation "God in the 21st Century" at the University of Oregon.

A recent event involving Catholicism filled the headlines. This was Pope Francis' six-day visit to the United States in September 2015. He was joyously welcomed by thousands of people. But it seems uncertain how Catholics viewed his proclamations.

Yet, for the purposes of this book, the new changes that Pope Francis has made in Catholicism seem to illustrate the flux that began to confront us all several decades ago. Perhaps this is a reflection of so-called "progress." Or is it simply a reminder of the vast differences between today and two thousand years ago? The following article likely will mean more to Catholics, but it may have implications for us all.

A "traditionalist Roman Catholic" in his own words, Judge Andrew P. Napolitano, wrote an opinion piece that appeared on Fox News. Judge Napolitano served as a New Jersey Superior Court Judge and teaches constitutional law as a Distinguished Professor at the Brooklyn Law School. His contribution seemed to reflect concerns expressed by many conservative Catholics.

"Without consulting his fellow bishops, the pope has weakened the sacrament of matrimony by making annulments easier to obtain [and] without consulting his fellow bishops, Pope Francis ordered that any priest may return those who have killed a baby in a womb to the communion of the faithful."

Judge Napolitano also reflected on changes in the Church during the 1960s and 1970s that "trivialized the Mass and blurred the distinctions between the clergy and the laity ... so as to make the Church more appealing and accessible to former and to non-adherents ... The result was a disaster ... Popes John Paul II and Benedict XVI attempted to roll this back ... Now here comes Pope Francis to use moral relativism to take the Church in two [other] dangerous directions."

In Pope Francis' speech to Congress, he tangentially referred to abortion and same-sex marriage by saying:

- "the Golden Rule ... reminds us of our responsibility to protect and defend human life at every stage of its development;" and
- "I cannot hid my concern for the family, which is threatened, perhaps as never before, from within and without. Fundamental relationships are being called into question, as is the very basis of marriage and the family."

It also seems important to acknowledge news media reports that religious evangelicals today consider books and personal accounts about so-called "near-death" experiences—especially about "visiting Heaven"—heretical to their faith. Moreover, they have publicly denounced any such accounts. As readers may know, the term "evangelical" seems to involve people who consider Holy Scriptures the verbatim word of God. Furthermore, that Jesus will actually return at the "End of Days" to resurrect and judge each person who has ever lived on earth. (I trust that this description is accurate. It is included here without any criticism.)

Although those claims apply to both Christianity and Islam—Muhammad told of receiving instructions from Allah through the angel Gabriel—Islam still does *not* include certain Christian beliefs. These include faith in salvation through belief that Jesus was God's sacrifice on the cross to save Gentiles from their original or inherited sin derived from Adam's fall in the Garden of Eden. Islam's disavowal apparently is because its Abrahamic (i.e., Judaic) background also does not believe in original or inherited sin, in salvation, in Jesus' divinity, or in the Trinity.

I apologize for that complicated explanation. You would find a much less complex yet informative discussion about this that a young divinity student dared to offer online in March 2015. He is Aaron Griffith, a doctoral student in American Christianity at Duke Divinity School. His article is, "Why evangelicals are divided by afterlife testimonials." His

article's online address is: http://www.religionnews.com/2015/03/26/
evangelicals-divided-afterlife-testimonials-commentary/

An Overlooked Attribute

It is important, before we leave this chapter, to mention an aspect of religion
that often appears in scripture readings, in hymns, and even in messages of
instruction and worship, but only by its name: the soul. For example, the
Apostle Paul wrote this about mortal death:

> "It is sown a natural body; it is raised a spiritual body. There is a natu-
> ral body, and there is a spiritual body." (KJV: 1 Corinthians 15:44)

The soul will be explored later as the key element in this book. I found that,
while religions seem to acknowledge the soul as a part of us, they never define
it as to its source, its purpose, or its nature. Yet this lack of details seems perfectly understandable: the soul has heretofore been elusive, even to the present day. Searches of ancient history revealed that Greek philosophers such as
Plato and Socrates addressed it in their writings and dialogue. Moreover, early
church fathers like Origen wrote about it. But for all of them too, the soul was
humanly imperceptible and inexplicable.

The next chapter instantly brings you forward almost two millennia,
from a world in which the Roman Catholic Church claimed that the Earth
is the center of our universe, to a seemingly ever-expanding cosmos in which
earth is now only *one* among 100 billion supposedly-habitable planets in *our*
Milky Way galaxy. Furthermore, astronomers at the University of Auckland
also claim that there are roughly 500 billion *galaxies* in the full universe, says
writer Sebastian Anthony.

Two

The "Other" Reality

*"From their experience or from the recorded experience
of others, men learn only what their passions and their
metaphysical prejudices allow them to learn."*

Aldous Huxley

The previous chapter took us back in time more than two thousand years, to trace the development of religion. You may remember that the Catholic Church maintained that the Earth is stationary—the center of our universe—and the Sun revolves around it. Not until the fall of 1992 did Pope John Paul II order a new look at evidence in Galileo's trial. He was acquitted, three hundred and fifty-nine years after his trial!

This illustration of human—and institutional—intransigence supports Aldous Huxley's admonition at the beginning of this chapter. This seems very appropriate since the book will expose you to many, almost mind-boggling, scientific, medical, and psychology claims that you may have missed. These are offered with reference not *only* to religion, however, but also to almost every view you hold about life and death. That latter term—death—is noteworthy, because, as the chapter title announces, even many scientists are increasingly sensing another, possibly coexisting, "reality." But, as you will discover, that "other" reality seems *intentionally* to remain humanly imperceptible and inexplicable—except for its *experiential* manifestations.

To get us started, have you or any of your friends ever had the following weird experience? It has happened to many people. Each of them found it quite disturbing. They were *unable* to shake the feeling because it involved a possible threat. So, imagine your calm being suddenly jarred by an uncanny sense that a loved one or close friend had a serious accident or even died unexpectedly. Your foreboding refused to leave, especially if you were thousands of miles away and out of touch. Only later, after you learned what *had* happened, you discovered that the accident or death occurred at *precisely* the time you first "felt" it. This is an example of a typical *adult* psychic experience.

Recall the *popularity* of books about sudden cardiac arrest survival and near-death experiences? That may have resulted from simple curiosity. But some readers may have secretly been looking for reassurance of an afterlife or Heaven. Of course, major world religions promise this, but with certain restrictions.

It therefore seems worth considering here that this "imperceptible and inexplicable" *other* reality just may include what we call "Heaven." I use the word "include" because I suspect that many readers would categorically *deny* that any such other reality might be an *all-encompassing and even limitless* "spirit world." But please notice, as you read through this book, how many ideas and concepts that just *might* apply to that kind of a "super-reality."

What Is "Real"?

Therefore for now, this book simply asks you to consider that "something more" *may* actually exist than what you can see, hear, touch, taste, and smell. You naturally are most comfortable with the people, things, and experiences you grew up with. Scientists may occasionally surprise you with what they learn. But this generally poses no threat unless they warn you, such as with Ebola. Therefore, when science *disavows* anything, such as strange phenomena that have happened down through many centuries, you typically doubt or even ignore those incidents.

For example, some young children may surprise you with their own kind of psychic ability. It comes unexpectedly for parents, who either ignore it or warn them "Don't tell anybody." Yet, the kids consider it normal. An actual example involves a seven-year-old girl named Jenny, riding in the back seat of their family car. She asked, "Mommy, if a man in a big truck, a man who can't speak English, bangs into our car and doesn't hurt us but smashes the car, do we have to pay to get the car fixed?" A few minutes later their car *was* hit by a dump truck, driven by a man who *couldn't* speak English. Jenny blamed herself, even though her mother simply ignored the warning.

However, psychology professor Tobin Hart carefully paid attention when his young daughter quietly asked, "Daddy, do you see the pretty lady?" at her bedtime one night. His book offers what he learned about some children's mystical experiences. It is entitled *The Secret Spiritual World of Children: The Breakthrough Discovery That Profoundly Alters Our Conventional View of Children's Mystical Experiences.*

Gallup keeps track of Americans' beliefs in the paranormal. In their recent poll, forty percent believe in extrasensory perception; thirty percent in telepathy; one in four in clairvoyance; and one out of five in reincarnation. Obviously, participants' responses are anonymous—no one would admit this to a neighbor or friend! David Moore provided the complete results.

Such tallies have a hallmark of the near-death experience (NDE): you can tell other people but you likely would *not* dare. NDEs and psychic events all reek of the unreal, bizarre, and even psychotic. This is especially true if the incident was in sharp contrast to "normal" reality. Thankfully, reports from NDE survivors are now given more credence. Researchers increasingly attribute near-death experiences to a kind of "consciousness" that *can survive* brain death. This will be discussed later in this book.

Recently, for anyone who *still* does *not* accept that explanation, a new kind of "experience" is being revealed around the world. These are called "shared-death experiences," since they typically involve *healthy* family members. An example is several family members attending the death of a loved one, as in a hospital or hospice room. The term "shared" indicates that *all* of them have an overwhelming "spiritual" experience during their loved one's death.

This may include an unearthly bright light even sprinkled with minute "star-drops," heavenly music, the "opening" of one wall of the room into "eternity," and a filmy shape of their loved one floating up from the bed and often being met by a similar figure of a deceased loved one, only to disappear together into the spiritual void as the wall "reappears."

A variation involves a close friend or family member who is lying beside the patient or holding his or her hands. The visitor briefly may be caught up with the loved one in a spiritually transcendent out-of-body "shared" experience as the patient dies, then the visitor "returns" to his or her own live body.

However, just as "near-death experiences" occur for only about one-fifth of all adult survivors of sudden cardiac arrest, "shared-death experiences" are not commonplace. Yet participants in both cases have no doubt about what happened. Researcher Raymond Moody, who first publicized "shared-death experiences," first heard about them *privately* from individual academic health professionals who *themselves* had such a disturbing personal experience with the death of his or her loved one. Moody and his family later had such a group experience with the demise of his mother.

You might ask, if "shared-death experiences" have occurred in the past, why hasn't there been more publicity about this? Would you have reported it? Most people who witnessed it years earlier probably were *unwilling* to admit it. Moreover, the news media has naturally been skeptical. Obviously, cynics disavow anything paranormal. Yet, the increasing awareness of "shared-death experiences" almost indisputably points to an inexplicable *source* of phenomena beyond what is called "normal reality."

Another source of *experiential* evidence included in this book, as close to being factual as seems possible, is the time-honored technique of psychotherapy: hypnotic regression. It traditionally has been used to uncover and treat traumatic early *childhood* memories as well as *repressed* memories, like sexual abuse and post-traumatic-stress-disorders.

Since the last quarter-century, however, it also has been used in thousands of cases of past-life and life-between-lives (i.e., "spiritual") hypnotic regression.

"Past lives" may seem implausible, but for two possible explanations. The first is reincarnation, which was a common belief in Jesus' time and was respectfully taught even at that time. The other is a hypothetical universal memory field.

Noteworthy, too, is the current use of hypnotic regression in our criminal justice system. Conducted under carefully structured protocols, it has proved worthwhile in obtaining criminal evidence from repressed memories in *present* lives.

In contrast to everything you read thus far, you may never have heard the term "scientific materialism." This is the belief that "reality" is only physical—just what you can see, hear, touch, taste, and smell. Mainstream science and academia jealously defend this "paradigm" against all non-believers, by disavowing all paranormal phenomena.

Science has operated for some time with the paradigm that materialism is the *only* reality. However, psychologist and researcher Charles Tart was among the first to publicly challenge this with his 2009 book *The End of Materialism: How Evidence of the Paranormal Is Bringing Science and Spirit Together*.

Science now realizes that some in their midst are advancing ideas about what is sometimes called "the unknown." But any academician who is *not* tenured recognizes the career risk of researching or publicizing anything beyond known or material subject matter.

Real "Material" Revelations

Yet, keep one apparent fact in mind as you read the following details about some recent scientific advances. Both mainstream science and academia have obvious pride in these "material" accomplishments and encourage you to be aware of them. The following therefore illustrate some breathtaking advances in the *physical world*. These would have disputed beliefs existing not only during the rise of religions but even just a hundred years ago.

Just consider the new theories that challenge even our "known" reality. For example, some astrophysicists believe that the Big Bang was *not* the "one time only" event as was previously supposed. In fact, to them the Big Bang may have been just one of hundreds, possibly thousands of similar events in a "multiverse" of an unknown number of universes. They speculate that the Big Bang was surely not the beginning of *all* matter but simply the creation of *our* universe. Princeton University's Paul Steinhardt and Neil Turok advanced this idea in their book *Endless Universe: Beyond the Big Bang.*

Another way to feel humble is to realize the number of stars in the *known* universe. As revealed by CNN, astronomers at the Australian National University estimate it to be ten times the number of grains of sand on Earth and eleven times the number of cups of water in all the Earth's oceans—70 sextillion or 7 followed by 22 zeros.

A NASA Discovery Mission named "Kepler" had found over a thousand planets whose temperature is habitable for liquid water and life. That project had also confirmed its first planet in the "habitable zone" of its host star. Known as Kepler-22b, that planet is about 2.4 times the radius of Earth and is 600 light years from Earth.

In an article by Ann Trafton "Life Beyond Our Universe" in a 2010 online *MIT News*, physicists theorize that life also may exist in universes with physical laws different from ours. Any persons who doubt this need only watch scenes from thousands of feet below the waves where deep ocean creatures have adapted to sulfides in place of sunlight, as detailed in the American Museum of Natural History online article "Black Smokers."

Now too, based upon the adaptation of deep ocean creatures on earth and reports of water found beneath the surfaces of other planets, scientists are cautiously suggesting the possible existence of at least primordial life in *those* underground waters. For example, scientists at the University of California at San Diego (UCSD) claim, "Life [there] might be a bit strange, but perhaps not a lot stranger than the life forms recently found around the hot vents in the abyssal ocean [here]." This appeared in their online article "Europa & Titan: Moons With Life?"

The "Unknown"

New scientific revelations have dramatically stretched the dimensions and characteristics of the cosmos beyond our wildest dreams. Moreover, new disclosures about the apparent nature of our subatomic material world add further uncertainties.

Perhaps most amazing, many scientists believe that beneath the veneer of visible physicality, there exists a world that typically is invisible and enigmatic yet is crucial to human life. Its almost infinitesimal units of matter, force, and light are composed of energy. But these units (i.e., quanta) are individually distinct rather than part of a continuous flow; they exist as particles and waves; and yet they have no place or state of existence *until* they are observed or measured. Before that, their location and physical characteristics are assigned probabilities.

What is equally fascinating, the action of a person or instrument focusing attention on a single quantum not only "fixes" the existence of that quantum but also instantly fixes the existence of a "twin" quantum into a complementary (i.e., opposite) state. This occurrence is based upon the twins having been connected (i.e., entangled) then separated by an *unlimited* distance before the research observation. Although quanta are invisible to human eyes, quantum mechanics have helped account for various otherwise inexplicable scientific hypotheses.

This *manifestation* of quantum *behavior* is therefore considered a *technically* observable phenomenon, although the underlying cause or force is *invisible*. In a sense, therefore, the term "experiential evidence"—which is used extensively later in this book—can be applied here to detectable evidence of quantum behavior. The term seems very appropriate for phenomena for which we *still* do not understand the source or cause.

These quantum manifestations therefore are believed to exemplify "fields," whereby field *effects* are technically observable even though the fields are not. A "field" might be considered an area of unknown characteristics that exerts influences on behavior within its range. Known examples include gravitational and electromagnetic fields. Moreover, a concept of "non- locality" is increasingly being found for fields. This applies whenever a field-effect transcends the physical constants of material reality.

Notably, world-renown scientist and futurist Ervin Laszlo claims that the increasing incidence of puzzles and anomalies accumulating in many disciplines is pushing science to develop a new paradigm—to acknowledge "the unexpected and often strange findings that stress the current theories of the physical world, the living world, and the world of human consciousness."

More recently, science's increasing emphasis on *material* reality and the boom in technology all contributed to disavowal and disregard for the "other" reality—until increasing *experiential* evidence started becoming available. Since the "other" reality is not normally perceptible to humans, this chapter was intended to stress the need for expanding our "what if" perspective of "reality" to include the *possibility* of the "other," yet still normally invisible and inexplicable, reality. Revelations from research in both the infinite and infinitesimal aspects of the *material* reality surely must stimulate eager imagination for the unknown and unseen mystery of the "other" reality.

This chapter should have helped you to at least contemplate that life involves much, much more than what you experience daily. Unfortunately for those who require *physical* proof in order to believe that anything is "real," they may be sadly disappointed in this life.

Now "secularism" grows openly with contemporary doubts about any purpose for life on earth beyond one's self and family, perhaps in the misconception that human life is final. Although "secularism" is now used even to justify strict separation between religions and government, the root word "secular" seems more precisely defined as "Worldly rather than spiritual," according to the Fourth Edition of the *American Heritage College Dictionary*.

Notice that this dictionary definition contrasts two states of human disposition: worldly and spiritual. Notably, the Autumn 2014 cover story of *The American Scholar* was entitled "Instant Gratification." Its author, Paul Roberts, asks in the article's subtitle, "As the economy gets ever better at satisfying our immediate self-serving needs, who is minding the future?"

But!

But before leaving this chapter's consideration of the *possibility* that any such "other" reality *may* actually exist, is it *not* reasonable—in the context of religion—that an "other" reality may be the spiritual realm of God and Heaven?

27

Furthermore, if God is eternal, therefore never changing, and we are *now* realizing how vast the "spirit world" actually *might* be, is it fair to wonder if God was ever *ours alone*?

Rather than immediately react to both of these questions, please *first consider* two reasons that seem to have eroded many, if not most, peoples' belief in God! First and most obvious, the "spiritual realm" is non-material and therefore will *always* be humanly imperceptible and inexplicable! Second, although many people will not *admit* it, they lost faith because God *did not* intervene in natural calamities and *did not* respond to their personal trust and fervent prayers for help! People probably felt *personally slighted* when they "knew" about the Hebrew Old Testament stories like the "manna in the wilderness," the "parting of the Red sea," and "Noah's Ark." Yet everyone was told, like I might have been, just have "faith!"

But please realize that the Old and New Testaments were never intended to be *literal history* books! Word of mouth (i.e., legends) remained the primary means of "publicizing" anecdotal accounts until the invention of the printing press around 1440 CE, and even then, source documents in Aramaic, Hebrew, Greek, or Latin often still had to be translated.

Next, you will be amazed how your "consciousness" is so much more than just your "waking" consciousness.

Three

CONSCIOUSNESS WITHIN YOU

*"Our normal waking consciousness ... is but one special type
of consciousness, whilst all about it, parted from it by the
filmiest of screens, there lie potential forms of
consciousness entirely different."*

WILLIAM JAMES

You already may know that you have a sort of "consciousness" that you
are *not* aware of and therefore you do not control. It also provides *no*
memories that you know of. This is called the "autonomic nervous system."
It automatically regulates your bodily functions like breathing, heartbeat, and
digestive processes.

"Waking" Consciousness

In contrast, your "waking" consciousness is the part of you that you know
very well. You realize that you have some degree of control over it and
that it is the source of memories that you typically *can* recall. But how
far back in your life can you remember something from your very early

29

childhood? For most people, it is not until *after* three to four years of age, or even later.

"Waking" consciousness has been believed to involve your brain. "Waking" means you are fully "aware" of everything that happens to you and around you, plus a variety of information, thoughts, questions, decisions, and the like. Therefore, what you see, hear, touch, smell, and taste through your five physical senses are made aware to your "waking" consciousness.

But *"waking" consciousness* is *not* located in a certain "center" of your brain. Rather, that consciousness depends upon coordination of billions of neurons in your brain with one another. During *unconsciousness*, by contrast, that neuron relationship becomes much less efficient, according to a recent UCLA report by its lead study author, Martin Monti. In general, these two contrasting mental states are similar to a light switch, "on" and "off."

Neuroscientist Christof Koch suggests that "waking" consciousness may be characteristic of an information-processing system, such as the brain, if it is sufficiently complex. This seems in agreement with the UCLA report, which reflects the integrative nature of the brain.

Probably the most important attribute of your "waking" consciousness is that you are *entirely* unique among all six to seven billion humans on Earth. No other individual has had an *exact match* of your life experiences. Generally speaking, this is especially true because your individual experiences not only created *conscious* memories. They also stored "hidden memories" of which you are *not* aware.

So this chapter introduces some "potential forms of consciousness entirely different" from the one you know best. Yet, as you may already know, science still cannot explain our "waking" consciousness. For readers who might be interested in the recent interdisciplinary background to the persistent enigmas about the mind and "waking" consciousness, an early 2015 online article in *the Guardian* is both entertaining and comprehensive. Written by Oliver Burkeman, it is appropriately entitled "Why can't the world's greatest minds solve the mystery of consciousness?"

Special Types of Consciousness

The eminent William James was known as an original thinker in and between the disciplines of physiology, psychology, and philosophy. He was the first educator to offer a psychology course in the United States. This chapter therefore will surprise you, as James suggests, with *two* "special types of consciousness" separate from your "waking" consciousness, both of which you are *not* aware. Neither are you aware of the "memories" they create, which are called "hidden," "unconscious," or "implicit." In addition, one of these "special types of consciousness" *also* has diverse *other* manifestations, that will be discussed in a later chapter.

But you obviously must wonder, "How and why would we have such unusual 'extra' kinds of consciousness in addition to our 'waking consciousness'?" This chapter will now discuss the "how" and "why" of *unconscious* memories from two recently acknowledged kinds of consciousness. The next chapter, in turn, will explore the *potential impact* of such unconscious memories at later times in a person's life.

Our Two Cerebral Hemispheres

Your "waking" consciousness creates memories of *all* your *conscious* experiences. Those are the memories you *can* recall, unless you suppressed them for any reason, typically from sexual abuse or other post-traumatic-stress.

But *both* your "waking" consciousness *and* those *memories* do *not* become possible until your "*left* cerebral hemisphere" becomes active around three years of age. Using dynamic single photon emission computed tomography and cerebral blood flow measurements, Chiron and colleagues found that the "left cerebral hemisphere" doesn't operate fully until that time. Then, the left one also provides what is called "cognition." These are brain faculties that make possible the many mental processes you use daily. The left one therefore becomes the dominant half in later years, apparently because of the fast pace of our lives and left hemisphere functions.

But an adjacent part of your brain—called your "*right* cerebral hemisphere"—becomes active earlier and is dominant up to three years of age. So just as you formed *conscious* memories after around three, you formed *unconscious* memories before that age. Both kinds of memories are created from your experiences, except the ones before three remain "hidden." For example, remember the earlier question, "How far back can you remember?" This is because most people *cannot* recall anything before age three.

Yet, if any of those earlier *experiences* were very emotional—fear of being left alone or feelings of not being loved, for example—those "hidden" memories also included *how you reacted* at *that* time. *Later conscious* experiences, as teens or adults, which cause *feelings for you* like those "hidden memories," might stimulate you to react or behave like you did then—without your knowing why!

So your brain stores "hidden memories" differently from "conscious memories." Technically, when both hemispheres are operating, the left hemisphere operates at a faster frequency (i.e., registered on an EEG) than the right, consistent with our busy daily lives and waking consciousness; and the right hemisphere operates much slower. *Overall* hemisphere operation therefore slows *very gradually* according our state of mind: active, relaxed, or meditative. Active: left only; relaxed: left plus right; and meditative: right only. But realize that this description is very simplistic, simply to illustrate general hemisphere operation—the range from "full" left to "full" right is very broad and change is very subtle.

Significance of Cerebral Hemispheres

The significance of the right cerebral hemisphere has only recently been acknowledged as *the key* to mental and physical health throughout our lives, according to research pioneer Allan Schore. He is a member of the clinical faculty of the Department of Psychiatry and Biobehavioral Sciences, UCLA David Geffen School of Medicine. The term "the unconscious" (i.e., right hemisphere) is sometimes attributed to the immensely influential psychoanalyst Sigmund Freud. He popularized the term without knowing exactly what it meant, before more recent advances in evolutionary biology and neuroscience.

However, in 2008, John Bargh and Ezequiel Morsella published a research summary of forty-eight scientific publications about "the unconscious." This confirmed that this neurobiological template for infant development (i.e., differential timing of hemisphere maturity) "permits cultural guides to appropriate behavior to be 'downloaded' during early childhood development. It greatly reduces the unpredictability of the child's world and his or her uncertainty as to how to act and behave in it."

In Allan Schore's 2010 publication entitled "The Right Brain Implicit Self: A Central Mechanism of the Psychotherapy Change Process," Schore writes, "It is the right hemisphere and its implicit functions … that are truly dominant in human existence. Over the lifespan, the early-forming unconscious implicit self [i.e., right hemisphere] continues to develop to more complexity, and it operates in qualitatively different ways from the later-forming conscious explicit self" [i.e., left hemisphere].

From the Womb and Birth

Medicine traditionally had considered the time before birth to hold little importance. This may have seemed reasonable considering that the fetus remains "undisturbed" in medicine's historic view and fetal studies are recent developments.

Toward the end of the last century, however, fascinating details began to emerge about fetal "memories." But "memories" from the womb certainly would *not* seem possible with fetuses' immature brains. Yet, as far back as 1979, psychotherapist Andrew Feldmar documented an unusual case. This involved four unrelated male teenage patients, who each had attempted suicide once a year at least five times. The time of year for each one's effort differed, yet for each the date remained the same for *every attempt.* Suspecting some link, the therapist did probing interviews with each of the four mothers. Each admitted having attempted abortion, ironically on about the same time of year that her son attempted suicide.

Although "hidden memories" from the womb may originate in a different way than "hidden memories" from the first three years after birth, both can have potential impacts later in life. Those four teenagers apparently had "sensed" that they were not worth living, but without realizing why. Yet admissions by the mothers to their sons ended their sons' suicide efforts. The psychotherapist concluded, "Once the [conscious] connection is made, the child is relieved of compulsively having to act out the [unconscious] memory."

Obviously, a single case like this is *not* sufficient to form a scientific conclusion. So a joint European study followed the children of thousands of parents for as long as *twenty-five years* after birth. This confirmed uterine memory and learning while answering age-old questions about how *threatened* abortion might later affect the mind and personality of the growing child. Unwanted children were matched with an equal number who were wanted, as acknowledged by parents of each child in the study. This book cannot possibly report all of the undesirable traits and the socio-behavioral and learning problems manifested by the *rejected* kids throughout the study, but those *negative* outcomes were relatively *absent* in children whose parents welcomed them. That study was published as "Born Unwanted: Developmental Effects of Denied Abortion" by Avicenum: Prague, 1988, and a Tenth Anniversary Review by David Chamberlain appeared in the December, 1998 issue of *Birth Psychology*.

If any readers still feel that memories from the womb must involve the fetal brain—even an immature one—a 2008 Swedish/French research project by Lagercrantz and Changeux entitled their report "The Emergence of Human Consciousness: From Fetal to Neonatal Life." Results were published the next year in the peer-reviewed professional journal *Pediatric Research*. The abstract says, " The fetus may be aware of the body, for example by perceiving pain. It reacts to touch, smell, and sound, and shows facial expressions responding to external stimuli. However, these reactions are probably preprogrammed and have a subcortical nonconscious origin."

Researchers in what is now called "prenatal (i.e., before birth) and perinatal (i.e., surrounding birth) psychology" differ in their designation for the source of such memories. However, they all agree that these memories exist; are impossible from an immature fetal brain; and therefore must represent one of William James' "potential forms of consciousness entirely different." A variety of terms have been used for the source: "fetal consciousness," "transcendent source of consciousness," and "soul."

Now there is increasing acceptance of *experiential* evidence manifested by emotionally traumatic memories from the womb and surrounding birth. Several quotes from literature in prenatal and perinatal psychology suggest that the *source* of such memories have advanced attributes. These include:

- "Birth memories contain so much wisdom and caring, analytical thinking and perspective, and other manifestations of higher consciousness, they raise fundamental questions about the nature of persons."
- "An innate mind, personal yearnings, spunk, spirit, and purpose. They can exhibit telepathy (i.e., thought communication), clairvoyance (i.e., seeing objects or events beyond the five senses), out-of-body perception, and transcendent awareness."
- "While brain matter has no explanatory power for such memories or any other manifestations of intelligence, emotion, or purpose during this time period, the evidence for consciousness remains pervasive and continuous. Thus, with no brain matter to explain them, memories continue to form and consciousness supports the human memories found at conception, shortly after conception, and the significant stream of events well before conception. Even more impossible to explain are the memories 'babies' display about interactions and relationships that occur over an extended period from months to years before the conception itself."

Regardless of your likely feelings of disbelief about what you have read so far, please form your conclusions about the entire book after you finish it. You still have many shocks and surprises to come!

The next chapter therefore examines the nature of the potential impacts of "hidden memories," some even shaping the offspring's thinking and behavior for a lifetime! But remember the two issues mentioned in the Introduction? You have just finished a prelude to the ""the now *documented* cause of rash acts by young people whose *very early* lives left them feeling *marginalized* in life. The next chapter examines the intended value of nature's plan and the multitude of opportunities for it to go wrong.

Four

Potential Impacts of Hidden Memories

"Man's task is to become conscious
of the contents that press upward
from the unconscious."

Carl Gustav Jung

*P*renatal and perinatal psychology researchers and practitioners have made amazing progress in detecting, analyzing, and treating emotionally traumatic memories from the womb and surrounding birth. But these claims *cannot* yet be made for the "hidden" memories that emerge from emotional trauma experienced between birth and three years of age.

Remember the conclusion of Bargh and Morsella's report that nature gives the infant up to three years before challenging it with "waking" consciousness and a myriad of accompanying cognitive responsibilities. In a sense the infant has a "private" time, of a sort, with its birth mother first, before it learns to accommodate to significant other persons and surroundings. This helps "reduce the unpredictability of the child's world and his or her uncertainty as to how to act and behave in it."

Obviously, newborns arrive *without* knowing what kind of world they face. Of course, parents may feel that infants will learn as they grow up. But some of this "learning" really can't wait until they "grow up." Yet babies do seem to fare much better in life if they develop some grasp of how to deal with *unpredictable* situations—and of course every *kind* of *new* situation is *unpredictable* at first! Remember too, it is the *nature* of their experiences that establish and reinforce their neurological "early-forming unconscious implicit self." Also, "over the lifespan, the early-forming unconscious implicit self continues to develop to more complexity, and it operates in qualitatively different ways from the later-forming conscious explicit self."

Not to belabor this explanation, but compare the way you "independently" developed the "self" you know so well, after your left hemisphere provided your brain faculties associated with "waking" consciousness. (You can review this in the final chapter.)

Infant Brains

Consider too, that at birth, our brains are the most *immature* of all our organs. The exquisite neurological architecture of the adult brain must be developed, and early life is therefore a period of unique sensitivity.

Relevant to this is Leslie Forstadt's article "Children and Brain Development: What We Know About How Children Learn." She explains that the newborn's brain has around 100 billion neurons (i.e., nerve cells)—all that the individual will *ever* have—and each neuron has around 2,500 synapses (i.e., junctions). By ages two to three, however, each neuron typically has developed about 15,000 synapses. Such connections help the brain develop "pathways" between different parts of their neurological system. Pathways are analogous to "communication cables." But in the brain they are developed *and* strengthened by *experience*—neurons that are *not* stimulated by use of these pathways therefore may be pruned.

Powers of Observation

But with changes in society's attitudes about parenting and childrearing, one thing often seems overlooked or disregarded. Or perhaps it *never* was recognized and acknowledged. Infants are *much* more perceptive than we may believe. With the world unfolding before them, *everything* is new. Even in their first year of life, babies have been shown to have powers of observation that *even* birth mothers may *not* recognize. This permits infants to detect *subtle* changes in things and people that may be oblivious to busy adults. This is stressed in a textbook by UC Berkeley psychology professor Alison Gopnik, *The Philosophical Baby: What Children's Minds Tell Us About Truth, Love, and the Meaning of Life.* The book's Amazon description says the book "explains the cutting-edge scientific and psychological research that has revealed that babies learn more, create more, care more, and experience more than we could ever have imagined. And there is good reason to believe that babies are actually smarter, more thoughtful, and more conscious than adults."

Birth Mother's Influence

The human being who is, by nature, the most influential person for the fetus and young child is his or her birth mother. Imagine living exclusively in seclusion with one individual for about nine months! But also realize that society seems to be encouraging birth mothers to spend less and less *quality* time with the child after birth. Consider, too, a total separation from the birth mother through adoption. Whether such a separation is anticipated could obviously affect the relationship between the birth mother and fetus. That relationship could be diluted substantially, as might happen with a "surrogate" mother.

Natural and adoptive parents typically consist of a female mother and a male father. This obviously enables the growing child to benefit by learning from both female and male role models. Of course, changing laws and societal practices now allow marriage of same-sex couples. So adoption authorities would be wise to take into account factors mentioned in this chapter when considering the welfare of the youngster in all adoptions.

Does all of this allow you to sense how we are moving *away from* parenting young people who would make this planet a more peaceful and happier place to live, for them and for us? Pepperdine University professor of psychology Louis Cozolino emphasized that our early relationships with our birth mothers can get us started in developing physiological and psychological systems that *will* withstand the rigors of life. Without this, we are left with less promising outcomes.

English psychotherapist Sue Gephardt's book, *Why Love Matters: How Affection Shapes a Baby's Brain,* complements Allan Schore's pioneering research. Never recognized until recent advances in neurobiology and neuroscience, that book's title succinctly captures the crucial significance of early emotional attachment between the baby and its birth mother. For example, when things go wrong with relationships in early life, the dependent child has to adapt; what we *now* know is that his or her brain adapts *too.*

Moreover, psychologist Kendra Cherry teaches that early *secure* attachment helps older children feel greater self-esteem, be more independent and self-reliant, perform better scholastically, have better teen and adult social relationships, and be less anxious or depressed. Remember the previously discussed joint European study that followed the children of thousands of parents for as long as *twenty-five years* after birth, and the outcomes for the wanted kids compared with the unwanted ones.

An Example

Maybe an example will help. Imagine looking into your baby's eyes. You may have a feeling of oneness with him or her. If you display a twinkle in your eyes, a wrinkled nose, or a bewitching smile, you may get a loving, even excited, response from your baby. He or she may even start a repertoire of facial expressions, body gyrations, and/or sounds. It seems like an encouraging mother-baby *emotional* exchange, which fosters attachment.

Suddenly, your cell phone rings. You turn aside to answer it. For a while, your baby may appear surprised. If you continue on the phone, he or she may attempt to get your attention. However, if you look away *long* enough, your baby may get frustrated and lose interest. He or she may eventually *avoid* renewing his or her interaction with you.

For each such situation, especially if repetitive, your baby may *reinforce* a "learned," unconscious memory-based reminder about how to react to similar unpredictable circumstances in the future. Consider, therefore, that an infant may have a collection of "reminders," some just deficits, for facing the future.

In an interview with Roz Carroll, Allan Schore deplored the fact that many birth mothers return to work when the infant is six weeks of age—yet this is when the infant is *just beginning* "face-to-face" joyful interactions.

Therefore, early relationships with parents, particularly birth mothers, can shape the child's future relationships with other people. Felt security is achieved or lacking, depending on early nurturing. Development of self-esteem can be encouraged or not, at a very early age.

Birth Mother As Absolute Authority

For the infant's first two to three years, imagine his or her feelings about the birth mother. Naturally, she was the child's most intimate human relationship for about nine months. During and following birth, therefore, the baby looked to her for security, love, and care. She must have been his or her "authority" figure. From earlier in this book, remember the impact that the four mothers' attempted abortions *unconsciously* had on their four sons? So it seems reasonable to conclude that offspring may form an *unconscious* and therefore *unchallengeable* view of their birth mothers as *infallible*. Strangely, this may be similar to how some of us view God. The child's view may even extend to *all* of his or her birth mother's words and actions, especially during those first formative years—if he or she is "good-for-nothing" or "bad," so be it in the child's view. Once established, however, the child's attitude simply may be perpetuated by the mother's future behavior. So her future improvement or even psychotherapy may fail to alter the youngster's firm conviction.

I base this section upon my beloved wife's strained relationship with her mother, which became obvious from our visits with her "sweet" mother. Betty became too fond of alcohol later in life and considered a rehab program, including visits with five different psychologists over time. But she bolted from the first appointment with each therapist when that male or female insisted on having her describe her relationship with her mother. When I once asked Betty to talk about her mother, she snapped back, "No! Never!" She carried a lifelong yearning for *any* expression of love from her mother, even a simple compliment. This may have been accentuated when my beloved Betty ran forward screaming during her mother's funeral and prostrated herself across her mother's coffin. I could only wonder at Betty's feelings.

Influences of Others

Other people will enter the young child's life. Naturally, his or her natural father might even become introduced during the pregnancy. Some fathers have discovered that the fetus sometimes will respond and even play games, during repertoires of touching the birth mother's belly, especially following certain patterns. It has been shown that the fetus recognizes the father's voice too. Siblings, relatives, and other caregivers will enter the baby's life, perhaps in that order. But, from the newborn or baby's point of view, however, recognize that "substitutes" will replace the "natural" birth family members in cases of adoption and "surrogate" birth mothers.

Have you ever noticed that older children who know or learn that they were adopted often feel "incomplete" in searching for their birth mothers? Could there be some elusive bond with one's birth mother? Or might there be a languished doubt, "Wasn't I worth keeping?" Remember from the previous chapter that hidden memories may significantly influence a person for his or her entire lifetime without that person's awareness.

UCLA clinical professor of psychiatry Daniel Siegel explains the connection between "implicit memories" (i.e., "the unconscious") and "awareness" in his book *Mindsight: The New Science of Personal Transformation*. He writes, "Recent discoveries in the field of brain science allow us to ... grasp how implicit memory can influence our present [life] without our awareness that something from the past is affecting us." This is of special significance when you understand that your *conscious* memories represent only a small fraction of "memories" stored within you.

For example, have you ever heard of "hot buttons"? These are *subconscious* (i.e., "the unconscious") sensitivities that can prompt you to react certain ways, typically without realizing it. But hot buttons can have a far less significant impact than some other subconscious memories embedded during early childhood.

However, secure relationships that infants develop with their birth mothers and with significant others build the foundation for emotional development and help protect children from many problems they may face growing up. But researchers have examined the life histories of children that succeeded *despite* many challenges. Study results have consistently found that these individuals had *at least one* stable, supportive relationship with an adult (usually a parent, relative, or teacher) beginning early in life.

Psychotherapy for Teens and Adults

Remember that one of the other two issues for this book is "the now *documented* causes of rash acts by young people whose *very early* lives left them feeling *marginalized* in life." Obviously, you are familiar with cases of teen suicide and with school or other institutional massacres by young people. But "Why would they do that?" you wonder. The answer that should *seem* likely to you *now* is the subject of this and the preceding chapter.

Naturally, whenever a teen or adult *realizes* that some unknown feeling or force has driven him or her to alcohol, tobacco, eating, or drug addiction—or a family member, friend, or physician discovers this—that detection may have been the reason for psychotherapy. Yet, *traditional* psychotherapy usually has involved patient thought processes arising from the left hemisphere, in other words "conscious" in some way.

Yet in Allan Schore's 2010 publication entitled "The Right Brain Implicit Self: A Central Mechanism of the Psychotherapy Change Process" he writes, " In the last ten years implicit unconscious phenomena have finally become a legitimate area of not only psychoanalytic but also scientific inquiry."

Adverse Childhood Experiences

The ACE (i.e., adverse childhood experiences) Study is likely the most extensive examination of the impact of abuse and dysfunction in early childhood upon teenagers at 18 years of age. Curiously, it was prompted by the *dropout rate* among *successful* participants in a Kaiser Permanente weight loss program in San Diego in the 1980's. Interviews with more than 200 of those *dropouts* revealed childhood problems that were the *source* of their obesity. But these were problems they *otherwise* felt *unable* to deal with than eating.

Therefore, more than 17,000 "middle-aged, middle-class Kaiser Permanente patients" were evaluated to determine degree of childhood exposure to "serious household dysfunction." Outcomes were assessed by patients' extent of exposure and their various attempts to resort to coping behaviors, including smoking and eating. Marcia Stanton discussed this situation in her article "How Early Experiences Impact Your Emotional and Physical Health as an Adult." As she suggests, however, correcting this is much easier to discuss than to implement. Unfortunately, contemporary attitudes toward child bearing and child rearing have become "modernized" to minimize parental responsibility and inconvenience.

Warrior Societies

As startling as the title of this section may be, it illustrates the significance of giving babies the "best" start in life. The following is based upon Timothy Taylor's book, as adapted by Patricia Torngren. Because warrior societies depended upon aggressive and violent traits in their men, "Colostrum [i.e., first breast milk, rich in antibodies] was frequently withheld from the baby. Early weaning usually followed this. As a result, the baby was left with unresolved pain, anger, helplessness and rage, which it could not understand and could not express. Later in life, this was likely to emerge in the form of either depression, or aggressive and violent tendencies, which might be projected onto, and acted-out against, another person, or a group of people." Thus, such a society encouraged war-like attitudes and behavior. Alice Miller's book offers the same conclusions.

Recent research seems to support the validity of the preceding claims. This involves the amygdala, the part of our brain known for stimulating the "fight or flight" response. It particularly reacts to emotions and anxiety, and therefore impacts social behavior, of which aggression is a key to warrior impulses. Notably, *cells* of the amygdala are mature at birth. This enables synapses to be formed according to an infant's experiences during the first couple of years. Moreover, research now shows that the amygdala's size and connections to other parts of the brain can increase through increased exposure to anxiety in the young. Christopher Bergland provided details.

Recent Research in Child Development

This rest of this chapter may appear excessively detailed or too "clinical." Yet researchers continue to discover *new* ways that human and other environmental (i.e., surroundings) influences during pregnancy, birth, and the first two to three years of life can contribute to later physical and mental diseases, as well as to "hidden" feelings of insecurity, disenfranchisement, and anger. Each influence that may involve a physical or mental disease outcome is mentioned here only for reference purposes, to enable readers who are further interested to follow up from the Bibliography. Yet, the following references *do* reveal a few of the intricate ways that brain development *can* respond to various stressful influences from caregivers or surroundings.

Before these and other such advances, most mental problems were addressed at detection and treatment stages. But advances in neuroscience and neurobiology are now enabling researchers to better link mental disorders and behavior with influences *on brain growth and development.*

Therefore, in addition to "hidden memories," research is discovering ways that *other* influences in our lives *during and after* infancy can affect brain development. During early life, for example, a new field of research has found that certain, often subtle, influences upon the infant can significantly *alter* the *intended* effects of his or her genes. This is called "epigenetics," since it does *not* change the infant's DNA but may *act* upon his or her genes.

This is illustrated in Rachel Barclay's 2014 article "Stress and Trauma in Childhood Affect Gene Expression for Life." She reveals how negative early-life experiences, such as abuse or the loss of a parent, can shape *how* the brain copes with *future* stress. For the scientifically curious, DNA is present in every cell of the body and contains genetic instructions for cell development and function. But gene "expression" (i.e., issue instructions) can be turned "on" or "off." This is just one of the many ways that epigenetics can negatively influence proper physical or mental development.

A specific example is offered by Sarah Romens, et al, writing in "Associations Between Early Life Stress and Gene Methylation in Children." Apparently, the general nature of children's environment can affect gene expression. High levels of stress can biochemically predispose gene expression to mental and physical disorders. Julie Markham and William Greenough's article expands on the effect of such influences "beyond the synapse."

But consider, too, that the prefrontal cortex is among the last parts of our brain to fully develop, reaching into our 20s and 30s. Yet it is the most evolved region of the brain, coordinating our highest-order cognitive abilities. It regulates our thoughts, emotions, and decisions through extensive connections with other areas of the brain, in performing so-called "executive functions." This term signifies, for example, the ability to distinguish between good and bad, assess possible consequences, and consider social acceptability.

Now some researchers believe that an unexpected growth spurt of synapses occurs in the prefrontal cortex just before puberty, with a pruning back during adolescence. Since both are experience-dependent, of course, that period must assume great significance in shaping teen-agers future lives and psychological risks. Amy Arnsten's article offers additional information, as does Sara Johnson, Robert Blum, and Jay Giedd's.

One of the most mother-friendly online sources for information about such influences and their potential impact on the fetus and the infant is BEBA (Building & Enhancing Bonding & Attachment) Center for Family Healing in Santa Barbara/Ojai, California. (http://beba.org). This site is offered in a Q & A format for seemingly every conceivable concern a mother might have. It covers prenates, newborn, and infants. The importance of BEBA's work is captured in their Web site claim, "The term 'birth trauma' specifically refers to adverse experiences one (i.e., newborn) has during birth, but any traumatic events that take place between conception and about the age of three have particular significance in shaping an individual's life." They add, "We are learning that stressful family events [and] emotional tension ... may also have long-lasting traumatic effects."

The Future

It may be obvious by now that parents hold the keys to the future of human-kind. Being told by many "experts" how to raise children, moms and dads may find it difficult to reconcile all that advice. Much of this is a generational matter, as earlier parents and grandparents insist that their offspring "turned out all right"! But who would dare criticize them?

Yet, consider that we eagerly welcome new wireless communications technology much more readily than we accept new discoveries about our offspring. Perhaps we seriously doubt that infants could possibly be "little humans," as psychoanalyst David Chamberlain claimed. Maybe it is just that new Internet conveniences help us navigate life more efficiently, while the surprises we are learning about parenting and rearing children seem more demanding. But where are our priorities?

Australian psychotherapist Robin Grille stretched our focus beyond our present opportunities in parenting to what we all could collectively achieve for the future. Her book *Parenting for a Peaceful World* rises above whatever prospective parents—and especially single expectant mothers—may feel and think about having a baby.

For example, everyone would likely doubt that prospective parents could have a substantial impact on future worldwide violence. Yet, you may surmise from this book that a supportive "unconscious" (i.e., subconscious) may reduce an offspring's negative, even malevolent, behavior later in life. Perhaps no better proof exists than the many follow-up studies involving fetal and early childhood trauma that produce potential lifelong behavior correlations.

It may be a young person's suicide because of cyberbullying or parental abuse, or an act of violence from accumulated aggression, as in "warrior societies." These and many other kinds of outward expression may reflect an inner lack of personal value, love, and security.

Suddenly, the Nigerian proverb "It takes a whole village to raise a child" assumes new meaning in light of what we are learning about the crucial significance of nurture in a fetus' and infant's early life. This awesome time becomes less of a repetitive obligation and more of an inviting opportunity for all caregivers in the young person's life.

Psychotherapy to uncover highly emotional or traumatic *subconscious* (i.e., "the unconscious") influences often requires hypnotic regression to help resolve their impact. Therefore, in the next chapter you will find that some kinds of such psychotherapy must reach beyond this material reality.

Five

PSYCHOTHERAPEUTIC AND ELECTIVE HYPNOTIC REGRESSION

"Hypnosis is the epitome of mind-body medicine.
It can enable the mind to tell the body how to react,
and modify the messages that the body sends to the mind."

JANE E. BRODY

This quotation from *The Possibilities in Hypnosis: Where the Patient Has the Power,* Jane Brody's article in the November 3, 2008 online issue of *The New York Times,* seems to bring the clinical value of hypnosis into modern times. Brody quotes clinical hypnotist Robert Temes, "Hypnosis cannot make people do anything they don't want to do."

Apparently Sigmund Freud was one of the early psychoanalysts to use hypnotic regression before turning to free association psychoanalysis. Yet, it now is employed too in our criminal justice system. Author F. J. Monaghan describes this in more detail in an online abstract from the National Criminal Justice Reference Service. There, as in *traditional* psychotherapy of early childhood and repressed memories of sexual abuse and PTSD, hypnotic regression may be the only way to obtain missing criminal evidence from certain witnesses.

During the latter part of the last century, however, patient care involving two eminent psychotherapists on opposite sides of the United States produced totally unexpected results and revolutionized hypnotic regression. This is best illustrated by the two actual case histories, which involved two academically rigid and professionally trained psychotherapists—who literally *stumbled* upon otherwise inaccessible information from their two patients.

The credibility of their subsequent research and publications rests in consistencies in tens of thousands of individually documented case reports. However, perhaps the best proof is that *even* a professional hypnotherapist may *misspeak* occasionally—as happened in the *accidental* instruction that each of these psychotherapists gave his patient during *traditional* psychotherapy.

Past Lives

Oral traditions and written legends around the world reveal that belief in reincarnation has existed from ancient times. It even was responsibly taught in Jesus time. Yet, the idea of *accessing* memories of "past lives" emerged only in the past quarter-century. Probably the first psychiatrist to publicize past-life hypnotic regression *unintentionally* discovered it with a patient named Catherine. As discussed earlier, hypnotic regression has long been traditional in psychotherapy for uncovering and treating emotionally traumatic past experiences during patients' *present* lives.

However, during one of Catherine's *traditional* sessions, she "flipped back" to a life thousands of years ago—*stunning* her psychiatrist! Rigidly academic in his training and practice, he could find *no* documented explanation for the patient's weird response. Later, however, after carefully reviewing her taped session repeatedly, he discovered that his instructions to her *might* have been *too* open-ended: "Go back to when you *first* felt this way."

The rest is history. Miami psychiatrist Brian Weiss now has successfully treated thousands of persons from all walks of life. These were intractable cases whose *present-life* mental or physical problems were unresponsive to any *other* known kind of treatment—other than "past-life" hypnotic psychotherapy.

So that you are *not* left wondering how hypnotic regression could possibly occur, the following description was offered by Brian Weiss: "The process is similar to watching a movie. The present-day mind is very much aware, watching, and commenting. The mind compares the movie's characters and themes with those of the current life. The patient is the movie's observer, its critic, and its star, all at the same time. The patient is able to use his present-day knowledge of history and geography to help date and locate places and events. Throughout the 'movie' he can remain in the deeply hypnotized state."

Although Weiss has published several books illustrating different aspects of past life regression therapy, one seems to capture the overall benefit best—*Through Time Into Healing: Discovering the Power of Regression Therapy to Erase Trauma and Transform Mind, Body, and Relationships.* He writes, "I have found that about 40% of my patients need to delve into other lifetimes to resolve their current life clinical problems. But when past-life therapy is used to bring these long-repressed memories to awareness, improvement in the current symptoms is usually swift and dramatic." Recall the four teenagers' repeated suicide efforts until they learned of their mothers' attempted abortions? Although their subconscious memories were from the womb, their conscious awareness resolved the problem.

Spiritual Hypnotic Regression

Just like Brian Weiss' shocking introduction to "past lives," the psychotherapist who discovered "life-between-lives" was caught blindsided by how it *first* happened. An academically rigid professional, he had been uncomfortable with "past-life" regression. Yet, this particular patient's unusual symptoms seemed to warrant its use. Even with her family members nearby, the older woman constantly complained of being "so lonely." But California's Michael Newton had no way to be prepared for the bizarre outcome of his effort.

During the patient's trance, Newton *inadvertently* mentioned the word "group" and the patient started crying. Newton asked her why. She blurted out, "I miss some friends in my group and that's why I get so lonely on Earth." Dumbfounded, Newton asked her where her group was located. "Here, in my permanent home," she explained, "and I'm looking at all of them right now!" The patient apparently was *very* hypnotizable and *mentally* had moved herself past the death scene in her previous life and *into* the afterlife (i.e., Heaven)! This was Newton's first, astonishing exposure to what was then called "life-between-lives" hypnotic regression.

After *eventually* realizing that his patient had accidentally tapped into "this mysterious place," Newton was intrigued "to find out for myself the steps necessary to reach and unlock a subject's memory of their existence [there]." So he dedicated a decade of research to "constructing a working model of the spirit world" (i.e., "life-between-lives" or Heaven).

He accomplished this by developing special questioning techniques to avoid "leading the witness." But he also recognized that the overwhelming nature of the experience could cause the patient or client to mentally dawdle. Newton therefore helped subjects keep pace by asking such questions as "your impressions," "anything unusual" (i.e., about visitors, surroundings, sounds, or colors), or "other activities" (i.e., recreation, learning, or serving). Newton subsequently published ten years of research involving seven thousand cases.

Colorado psychologist Linda Backman co-established The Society for Spiritual Regression with Michael Newton, which is now known as the Newton Institute for Life-Between-Lives Hypnotherapy. Backman has conducted more than one thousand past-life and life-between-lives hypnotic regressions. Her book offers a wealth of her patients' first-hand accounts.

The Institute's book is a collection of representative life-between-lives hypnotherapy cases from thirty-two psychotherapist members of the Institute around the world. That book is significant in illustrating the global unanimity of life-between-lives hypnotic regression results. Institute members now practice in North and South America, Europe, Asia, South Africa, and Australia. The Institute's Website offers a search-by-country option for finding member Institute-certified psychotherapists for the three-to-four-hour session (newtoninstitute.org).

You naturally may question the trustworthiness of these patients' and clients' testimonies. According to Newton, however, "Subjects cannot lie, but they may misinterpret something seen in their *unconscious* mind just as we do in the conscious state. In hypnosis, people have trouble relating to anything they don't believe is the truth."

Past Life as Prelude to Spiritual Hypnotic Regression

Since some of you may have participated in a past-life regression, it is important to realize why anyone pursuing a "life-between-lives" regression should first *begin* any such session with a past-life regression. This obviously helps account for the three-to-four hours required. But it also offers a "natural" trance progression.

During a "life-between-lives" hypnotic regression, the death scene in a hypnotized previous life is as close as possible to replicating the soul's transitional experience following actual physical death. Moreover, the past-life trance approach should be less problematic for the patient or client than an abrupt introduction to the spirit world. This also enables the subject to become comfortable first with his or her past life, typically in just an earlier time frame.

Yet, this sequencing also affords another advantage if the past life contained unexpected trouble areas. Past-life imprints of any such difficulties would likely go undetected if the session had proceeded directly to the spirit world. However, the psychotherapist can determine how to handle any such past-life trauma and maintain the subject's composure.

Spirituality and Psychiatry

You likely will doubt the authenticity of this section heading—linking a still uncertain state of mind with a distinguished branch of medicine. But I stumbled across a book with this title published by the Royal College of Psychiatrists in London in 2009! It was prepared by the RCP Spirituality and Psychiatry Special Interest Group and can be accessed online at http://www.psychiatry. ru/siteconst/userfiles/file/englit/%5BChris_Cook%5D_Spirituality_and_ Psychiatry%28BookFi.org%29.pdf. For example, members of this group have published papers on the potential present-life mental impact of past-life trauma, given the inability of science to disprove reincarnation. One of these by Marcel Westerlund is included in the Bibliography.

The "Border"

Later in the book you will learn a significant difference between spiritual regression and near-death experiences. Of course, the former occurs through hypnosis of a patient or client into a state of consciousness involving the right hemisphere. The latter typically occurs when a victim of sudden cardiac arrest reaches the second state of the near-death experience. But the former allows exploration of all of the soul's *memory* of its experiences in the afterlife, while the latter restricts the soul consciousness from "crossing the border" (i.e., exploring *past* the time of his or her cardiac arrest in the *present* life).

The following chapter discusses survival of sudden cardiac arrest. Many of those victims have an out-of-body experience and describe perceptions of their resuscitation.

Six

SURVIVAL OF THE SOUL IN CARDIAC ARREST

*"All truths are easy to understand once they are discovered;
the point is to discover them."*

GALILEO GALILEI

*P*robably the most-often debated claim in metaphysical experiences is the cardiac arrest survivor's "visit to Heaven," especially since those patients feel it is "more real" than their everyday life. Imagine what a revelation it would be—particularly for the more than twenty-two million near-death survivors—if their "visits" *actually were* the kind of preview of Heaven that we all would eventually experience when our bodies die! Remember that survivors' heart, lungs, and brain are shut down but soul consciousness survives, just as it does in mortal death. Remember, too, the legendary Canadian neurosurgeon Wilder Penfield's conclusion that the mind (i.e., soul consciousness) seems to have a source of energy apart from the brain.

Canadian psychiatrist Joel Whitton and Joe Fischer's book *Life Between Life* contains a revealing life-between-lives description from his electronics engineer patient. The man's account describes certain aspects of his experience that may be more typical than not in both near-death experiences and life-between-lives hypnotic regression. Usually, these hypnotic regressions take clients back to a past life, through the death scene in that life, and into the life-between-lives.

The patient said:

"In experiencing a past life, one sees oneself as *a distinct personality* which engenders an emotional reaction. In the interlife [i.e., life-be-tween-lives], *there's no part of me that I can see*. I'm *an observer sur-rounded by images*."

Certain words here seem especially supportive that each such experience is perceived by the soul consciousness. Whitton observes: "The awakening to disembodied existence is where the life-between-life [i.e., life-between-lives] really begins."

The psychiatrist elaborates with: "The inception of metaconsciousness [i.e., soul consciousness] produces drastic change in a subject's countenance. Every frown, every grimace, every intimation of fear, anxiety, and pain that had accompanied the death experience [of the past life] drains away to leave the face at first expressionless, then peaceful and relaxed and, finally, suffused with wonderment. The eyes may be closed but there's no mistaking that the subject is captive to enthralling visions. When he [i.e., Whitton] next com-municates with the person lying on his couch, he is talking, not to the per-sonality before him, but to the eternal self which has produced that temporal personality."

Survival of Sudden Cardiac Arrest

One thing that NDE experiencers eventually realize is how fortunate they were to survive. The number of deaths each year from sudden cardiac arrest is roughly equivalent to the number who, in total, die from Alzheimer's disease, assault with firearms, breast cancer, cervical cancer, colorectal cancer, diabe-tes, HIV, house fires, prostate cancer, suicides, *and* motor vehicle accidents *combined!* But with quick attention, proper cardiopulmonary resuscitation, possibly defibrillation, advanced cardiac life support, and, sometimes, mild therapeutic hypothermia, victims have been able to recover successfully. Maybe their loved ones, friends, and associates did *not* fully appreciate this!

Consider suddenly being "knocked out" at work or in a social gathering and "finding yourself" looking down on your body! No one else can see you or hear you, if you try to communicate, even though you can even "sense" other peoples' thoughts. That is about as close as anyone can come to death from sudden cardiac arrest yet still *possibly* recover.

Whether NDE survivors consider it a "bonus" to also "visit Heaven," that second stage may account for the "transformation" they experience. As mentioned earlier, not every sudden cardiac arrest survivor has a "near-death experience." Moreover, fewer still seem to "visit Heaven."

However, *complete* recovery still is far less promising than most people realize. A cascade of complicating factors can arise, particularly depending on the length of time that brain anoxia occurs, before restoration of the heartbeat and oxygenated blood reaches the heart and brain. Brain cells may already have initiated defensive mechanisms. Recognition and proper clinical management of these and other factors therefore *are* crucial to survival and *possible* recovery.

Obviously, therefore, having a "full" near-death experience is *not* a "piece of cake." So, even for those survivors who have *not* been ridiculed, chastised, or cast out for their NDE testimonies, their sense of camaraderie at NDE gatherings must seem like a homecoming reunion!

Support From A Controlled Surgery

One particular near-death experience supports claims that soul consciousness is the source of these events. These events certainly qualify as experiential evidence too for the idea that *soul consciousness survives mortal death*. Therefore, soul consciousness is not affected by shutdown of the brain, lungs, and heart *as was required* for this unique surgical procedure.

This was the unusual case of Atlanta composer/singer Pam Reynolds, who suffered from an aneurysm (i.e., ballooning) in the giant basilar artery deep inside her brain. Reynold's experience is described in Mario Beauregard and Denyse O'Leary's book *The Spiritual Brain: A Neuroscientist's Case for the Existence of the Soul.*

The credibility of Pam's near-death experience was strengthened by almost inoperable conditions that required draining blood from her head and lowering her body temperature to sixty degrees (i.e., normal is 98.6). Initially, Pam reported an out-of-body experience before meeting with her deceased relatives. Her later testimony was consistent with those reported by other survivors of out-of-body (OBE) and near-death (NDE) experiences. Reynolds was even able to accurately describe the saw used to cut through her skull—out of her normal line of vision. This is verifiable and potentially reproducible validation of the OBE component of the NDE.

A similar OBE is also reported by many of the eighty percent of cardiac arrest patients who don't have a full near-death experience. Kenneth Ring and Sharon Cooper's book, *Mindsight: Near-Death and Out-of-Body Experiences in the Blind,* offers a fascinating discussion about this. The authors wrote, "They have access to a kind of expanded supersensory awareness that may in itself not be explicable by normal means."

Blind patients have had both kinds of experiences, demonstrating that their brains were not involved. OBE survivors—both sighted and blind—often describe the emergency team members and procedures—correctly—sometimes even the instruments used and/or numbers registered on clinical status monitors. OBE survivors even report dust on tops of emergency room lights from their usual out-of-body viewpoint up near the ceiling! Medical team members later validated patients' observations.

NDE Simulations

Two purported simulations of near-death experiences have been reported. One is an experimental apparatus called the "God Helmet," whose weak fluctuating magnetic fields were claimed to induce "mystical experiences and altered states." The other is the near-black-out experience of fighter pilots being spun in a gigantic centrifuge to test and train them for high-speed jet aircraft. Both of these, involving live people, failed to evoke the core NDE experience.

NDE or ADE?

Critical care and resuscitation specialist Sam Parnia's 2013 book *Erasing Death: The Science That is Rewriting the Boundaries Between Life and Death* is a ground-breaking progress report on improving the outcome of cardiopulmonary resuscitation (CPR) for cardiac arrest and strengthening the chances of patient recovery.

Perhaps an analogy is necessary to emphasize that simple CPR may be *insufficient.* If electricity is abruptly shut off for a machine, all the machine parts halt operation. Restoration of power typically restarts the machine and it operates properly. Consider the difference between a machine and a human body. The body is composed of cells, tissues, and organs, each of which is far different from the parts of a machine. Biology 101 illustrates the individual nature of human "parts" and each part's "life of its own." CPR may therefore need to quickly acknowledge and address brain cell deprivation of oxygen and nutrients, which can cause cellular malfunction and initiate brain cell deterioration.

Parnia explains, "There has been a growing recognition that people who have had a close brush with death or have gone beyond the threshold of death and entered the grey zone that exists between death and permanent irreversible brain damage have provided consistent mental recollections that correspond with that period. Although most [people] still call these experiences NDEs, from my research and work I have determined that they are actual-death experiences or ADEs—[these patients] are not near death but have actually died."

Parnia continues, "If the mind—consciousness (or soul)—can continue to exist and function when the brain does not function after death, then it raises the possibility that it may be a separate undiscovered scientific entity that is not produced through the brain's usual electrical and chemical processes. Since 2000, some researchers, including me, have started to focus more on the cognitive experiences that people have during a cardiac arrest and hence death. This is no longer ambiguous and vague. Today it is becoming much more difficult to define or understand death without considering a person's consciousness or soul."

Psychic Experiences of the Incarnated Soul

Testimonies like Pam Reynolds' sound remarkably similar to what might be expected of "soul consciousness." In cardiac arrest (i.e., brain, heart, and lung shutdown), the soul consciousness part of us remains "alive" (i.e., energized)— remember: it survives physical death. Although incredible, the actual-death experience (ADE) apparently provides these patients a transcendent opportunity seemingly like that which each of us can expect at our mortal death. End-of-life experiences (ELE) will be discussed in a later chapter.

ADEs therefore may be *actual* "previews" of the afterlife being "viewed" through soul consciousness! ADE survivors' "visions" of Heaven could be just as real as their validated observations of the medical team members and re-suscitation process during their out-of-body (OBE) experiences. Although invisible to others, these survivor perceptions offer *experiential evidence of the psychic capabilities that soul consciousness demonstrates.*

This therefore distinguishes ADEs from experiences of *live* persons undergoing past-life (PL) and life-between-lives (LBL) hypnotic regression. Verbal testimonies from PL and LBL subjects suggest that these are from soul *memories of the afterlife housed in the sub- and superconscious minds* that can be communicated to the hypnotherapist.

Remember that these patients or clients retain verbal communication ability wherein focus has been shifted from their left to their right cerebral hemispheres. Using Weiss' earlier description of hypnosis, imagine yourself caught up in the emotional intensity of watching a captivating movie in which you are also the star, yet able to comment to a fellow viewer without disrupting your involvement in the movie.

Moreover, near-death (i.e., actual-death) survivors often claim that the awareness they feel and perception they have of "visiting Heaven" exceed their normal waking consciousness. Non-sighted patients speak about "seeing" for the first time. Some speak of spherical "vision," being able to see in all directions simultaneously. Some described the experience as "all-knowing," with a much-expanded awareness.

Remember again fetuses' special abilities that Chamberlain discovered among womb memories from his hypnotized patients: extrasensory perception, telepathy, clairvoyance, out-of-body perception, and transcendent awareness. If fetal consciousness *is* soul consciousness, and if soul consciousness is the origin of waking consciousness, some of these mental feats have heretofore been falsely claimed for the brain.

Remember the example early in this book of suddenly feeling that a loved one or close friend has been hurt or died? Such incidents often make it appear that the universe has an "information" grid or force field of some sort with which soul consciousness is associated. This seems to make so much sense that many books have proposed it. One is the transpersonal psychologist John James' book *The Great Field: Soul at Play in a Conscious Universe.* Another is the eminent scientific visionary Ervin Lazlo's book *Science and the Akashic Field: An Integral Theory of Everything.* These seem consistent with new discoveries in quantum mechanics and particle/wave theory.

In support of this idea, Michael Newton writes the following in the book *Memories of the Afterlife:* "Scientists are learning that subatomic particles, acting under the influence of vibrational energy waves, both record and store all images, animate and inanimate, on Earth. Events represent patterns of pure vibrational energy so that no human experience is ever lost that cannot be recovered for analysis in the timeless afterlife."

Coma

Researchers now consider coma in a new light. Their discoveries seem to support the presence of soul consciousness as part of our waking consciousness in everyday life as well as its continued existence when the brain is shut down. Coma typically involves patients on a medical ventilator, a machine designed to move breathable air into and out of the lungs of patients who are physically unable to breathe sufficiently on their own. If the patient's heart is pumping satisfactorily, even if it has had to be re-started, the ventilator typically should help his or her circulatory system to carry oxygenated blood to the heart and brain.

Depending upon how long the heart and brain have been without oxygen, the heart may re-start upon resuscitation but brain damage may have begun. That is why proper emergency room care is vital as soon as possible after CPR to sustain the heart's pumping action. Despite brain damage, the ventilator usually can help support the patient in a coma by supplying the heart with oxygenated blood.

Parnia's book contains several illustrations of critically ill patients who became comatose either from their condition or from induction by the medical team. Certain ones remained "alive" through life support and amazingly reawakened years later.

So Parnia asks, "Does consciousness, the self, or the soul become lost, in the true sense of the word, immediately after death? The answer," he says, " that is coming out more and more seems to suggest that it doesn't. Consciousness or the soul, while down and thus invisible to the outside world, is not lost forever as an entity."

The next chapter explores the details of the so-called "near-death experience" (i.e., actual-death experience) that some sudden cardiac arrest survivors describe.

Seven

WHAT NEAR-DEATH EXPERIENCES REVEAL

*"Death when unmasked shows us a friendly face
and is a terror only at a distance."*

OLIVER GOLDSMITH

This is a lengthy chapter. But it covers the many aspects of experiential evidence of our souls which exist in addition to those just discussed from hypnotic regression. First, let's examine two real-life examples of the out-of-body stage of near-death experiences that are *totally* indisputable by skeptics.

Note: this is a chapter that addresses one of the two *other* objectives of this book cited in the Introduction: "the brash *willingness* by terrorists to seek death for *false* promises of reward in Heaven." See also the section in this chapter "From Other Cultures."

Beyond Skeptics' Challenges

Skeptics have advanced many purported "material" explanations for near-death experiences. Since the out-of-body first stage seems more common than the second, it is important to acknowledge an out-of-body characteristic that *no* one has yet been able to challenge. It is the verifiable "observations" which these survivors often claim to have made while in sudden cardiac arrest. These include details of the resuscitation procedure, appearance of medical team members' clothing, comments made by team members, and even specific numbers on patient status monitors. Often, some of these items were outside of the patient's view or his or her eyes may have been covered.

Naturally, disbelievers still insist that being "unconscious" may permit some degree of perception by the patient. But some survivors *also* describe *another* part of their experiences that certainly remains *indisputable*! To understand this, first consider that the observations that survivors describe about their surroundings claim to be made from an "out-of-body" state *usually* near an upper corner of the room. But the exception to *any* challenge is that some patients' "spirit" does *not* remain in the room! Since this obviously seems inconceivable, here is a classic example whose details were verified.

It occurred while pediatrician Melvin Morse was an intern in pediatrics in a small town in Idaho. A seven-year-old named Katie had been found floating face down hours earlier in a community swimming pool. In the blunt jargon of emergency room physicians, she was a "train wreck." Miraculously, she recovered. Equally or more surprising, she told Morse that she watched her parents and brothers in their home, apparently before they had been notified. Morse described what she did:

"Katie wandered through her home, watching her brothers and sisters play with their toys in their rooms. One of her brothers was playing with a GI Joe, pushing him around the room in a jeep. One of her sisters was combing the hair of a Barbie doll and singing a popular rock song. Katie drifted into the kitchen and watched her mother preparing a meal of roast chicken and rice. Then she looked into the living room and saw her father sitting on the couch. Later, when Katie mentioned this to her parents, she shocked them with her vivid details about the clothing they were wearing, their positions in the house, and even the food her mother was cooking." This was from Melvin Morse's 1990 book with his kind permission.

Another real-life example seemed to complement Katie's experience—but this one offered the survivor's vivid *recall* about literally *every* aspect of his experience. It was orthopedic surgeon Anthony Cicoria's 1994 "out-of-body" experience after being struck by lightning at an outdoor park during a family birthday gathering. This is quoted from the July/August 2014 issue of *Missouri Medicine,* The Journal of the Missouri State Medical Association, with their kind permission:

"I ambled around the building to the pay phone and dialed my mother's familiar number, but there was no answer. With my left hand I pulled the phone hand piece away from my face to hang it up. When it was about a foot away from my face, I heard a deafening crack. Simultaneously I saw a brilliant flash of light exit the phone hand piece I was holding. A powerful bolt of lightning had struck the pavilion, traversed through the phone striking me in the face, as its massive electrical charge raced to ground.

"The force of the lightning blast threw my body backwards like a rag doll. Despite the stunning physical trauma, I realized something strange and inexplicable was happening. As my body was blown backwards, I felt 'me' move forward instead. Yet I seemed also to stand motionless and bewildered staring at the phone dangling in front of me. Nothing made sense.

"Suddenly, I realized what was going on. A motionless body was lying on the ground some ten feet behind me. To appearances the person was dead. To inspection the person resembled me. To my astonishment another look confirmed it was me! I watched as a woman who had been waiting to use the phone dropped to her knees and began CPR. I spoke to the people around my body but they could not see or hear me; but I could see and hear everything they did and said. It suddenly occurred to me that I was thinking normal thoughts, in the same mental vernacular I had always possessed. At that moment I suddenly had one simple, ineloquent and rude thought, 'Holy shit, I'm dead.'

"This cosmic realization of consciousness meant that my self-awareness was no longer in the lifeless body on the ground. I, whatever I was now, was capable of thought and reason. Interestingly there was no strong emotion accompanying my apparent death. I was shocked, certainly, but otherwise I felt no reaction to what should have been the most emotional of life's events. I saw no point in staying with my body, so my thoughts then moved to walk away. I turned and started to climb the stairs to where I knew my family still was.

"As I started to climb I looked down at the stairs like I would normally do. I saw that as I reached the third stair, my legs began to dissolve. I remember being disconcerted that, by the time I reached the top of the stairs, I had lost all form entirely and instead was just a ball of energy and thought. My mind was racing frantically trying to record and make sense of what was happening. Instead of bothering with the stairs, I passed through the wall into the room where everyone was. I went over to my wife who was painting children's faces. I had a clear realization that my family would be fine. Dispassionately, I departed from the building.

"Once outside, I was immersed in a bluish white light that had a shimmering appearance as if I were swimming underwater in a crystal clear stream. The sunlight was penetrating through it. The visual was accompanied by a feeling of absolute love and peace. What does the term 'absolute love and peace' mean? For example, scientists use the term absolute zero to describe a temperature at which no molecular motion exists—a singular and pure state. That was what I felt; I had fallen into a pure positive flow of energy. I could see the flow of this energy. I could see it flow through the fabric of everything. I reasoned that this energy was quantifiable. It was something measurable and palpable. As I flowed in the current of this stream, which seemed to have both velocity and direction, I saw some of the high points and low points in my life pass by, but nothing in depth. I became ecstatic at the possibility of where I was going. I was aware of every moment of this experience, conscious of every millisecond, even though I could feel that time did not exist. I remember thinking, 'This is the greatest thing that can ever happen to anyone.'

"Suddenly, I was back in my body. It was so painful. My mouth burned and my left foot felt like someone had stuck a red-hot poker through my ankle. I was still unconscious, but I could feel the woman who was doing CPR stop and kneel beside me. It seemed like minutes before I could open my eyes. I wanted to say to her, 'Thank you for helping me.' Nonsensically, all that came out was, 'It's okay, I'm a doctor.'"

No doubt you read Anthony Cicoria's experience either with your jaw dropped or in denial of its authenticity. Yet, he holds both MD and PhD degrees and, therefore, is both a surgeon and a scientist. Moreover, he prepared his full-length article "My Near-Death Experience: A Telephone Call From God" to be a part of the July/August 2014 issue of *Missouri Medicine*, The Journal of the Missouri State Medical Association. It therefore was *not* intended for lay audiences.

His full-length article later acknowledges the multitude of such reports from around the world, as well as efforts from the scientific community to replicate experiences having some similarities. Yet, Cicoria concluded, "What is clear to me is that my consciousness survived death, and I was able to verify details of my near-death and out-of-body experience that I would have no conceivable way of knowing except through conscious travel of my spiritual self outside of my body."

Notably, that special issue of *Missouri Medicine* was headlined "Getting Comfortable With Death & Near-Death Experiences" and was described as "[This] series will be the most encyclopedic and up-to-date in the world's literature."

However, if you search your computer for references to Anthony (Tony) Cicoria, what you will likely find is his *new* insatiable interest and ability in piano music! The word "new" means that before his sudden cardiac arrest, these did not exist for him! Could his "soul consciousness" have been stimulated to recover a past-life memory/skill?

Anthony Cicoria's detailed account of his out-of-body experience (OBE) seems to illustrate concepts in this book. However, if you have heard anyone *else* describe his or her OBE, you will recognize that Cicoria's summarized description as follows is exceptionally and uniquely complete, far different from the typical OBE account:

- "As my body was blown backwards, I felt 'me' move forward instead."
- "I had lost all form entirely and instead was just a ball of energy and thought."
- "It suddenly occurred to me that I was thinking normal thoughts."
- "I, whatever I was now, was capable of thought and reason."
- "The people around my body could not see or hear me."
- "But I could see and hear everything they did and said."
- "This cosmic realization of consciousness meant that my self-awareness was no longer in the lifeless body on the ground."

NDE Survivor Perceptions

For those who are *not* familiar with perceptions that near-death survivors typically describe from their core experience, this is the stage that *includes* the so-called "visiting Heaven." The following list therefore was prepared from several sources. However, not every step is experienced with every second stage NDE:

(1) Departing from the physical body;
(2) Viewing the physical body from an elevated position;
(3) Moving away and up through a "tunnel";
(4) Feeling peace and quiet;
(5) Welcoming by the "white light";

(6)   Sensing repair of any disabilities;

(7)   Meeting deceased relatives, friends, and others;

(8)   "Watching" a life review;

(9)   Having a sense of ineffability;

(10)   Being refused admittance beyond the "border"; and

(11)   Returning to the physical body.

NDE Survivor Conversions

If you are not familiar with the second stage of many near-death experiences (NDEs), this chapter also reviews the most-consistent outcomes from so-called "visiting Heaven." The usual impact upon NDE survivors of sudden cardiac arrest is quite pronounced. They typically undergo a radical transformation of attitudes about life on Earth:

- Much greater appreciation for life itself.
- Deeper sense of wonder and gratitude about living.
- Greater self-esteem and self-confidence.
- Compassion and understanding for everyone.
- Stronger reverence for life in all of its forms.
- Disavowal of competitive and materialistic pressures.
- Caring and concern for others.
- Personal certainty about the existence of God.
- No longer fear death.

Yet these lasting effects on the survivor often cause grave concern for his or her spouse, family, friends, and business associates—instead of inspiring awe and gratitude for the victim's survival! Obviously, their apprehension typically occurs because such alterations frequently contrast sharply with the survivor's previous personality and with the "normal" beliefs and behavior of those around him or her.

From Other Cultures

A recent study among Iranian Shiite Muslims adds a significant dimension to a database developed by Jeffrey and Judy Long about the effects of near-death experiences, which you will see later. Jeffrey Long was one of a four-member research team headed by Alinaghi Ghasemiannejad, which reported the study results in the Fall 2014 *Journal of Near-Death Studies*. Excerpts from the abstract seem noteworthy here:

- "Though an early researcher concluded that Muslim NDEs appeared to be rare, later authors concluded that they may be common and that their key features may not be very different from those of Western NDEs."
- "Eight prominent features of Western NDEs were present in our participants' NDEs, and, like Western NDErs, our participants often reported profoundly positive changes in attitudes, values, and spiritual beliefs following their NDEs."

Children's Testimonies About NDEs

Several NDE researchers point to the nature of young children's NDEs as *unchallengeable* evidence of the authenticity of the phenomenon. *These young people describe their NDE experiences with an innocence and freshness not often found in adults. Youngsters reveal a viewpoint not yet colored by religious or societal influences. It is indeed unlikely that they have ever heard of near-death experiences.* So kids' testimonies provide a convincing baseline for the validity of NDEs that is amazingly matched by adult NDE survivors. The main difference between the two seems to be the adults' preconditioned identification of the "white light" as a familiar religious figure. Adults also may meet loved ones who had died *without* the NDE survivor's knowledge and children may be greeted by previously-deceased siblings of whom they were *not* aware.

For example, a poignant story in eminent psychiatrist Elizabeth Kubler-Ross' book *Life After Death* involved a twelve-year-old girl. She did not share her near-death experience with her mother. The daughter had found it nicer there (i.e., Heaven) than at home and wanted to stay, but she was told she had to go back. Later, her excitement about her experience drove her to tell somebody, so she confided in her father. "What made it very special, besides the whole atmosphere and the fantastic love and light," the child said, "was that my brother was there with me and he hugged me with so much love." But after a long pause, the child complained, "The only problem is that I don't have a brother!" Her father started to cry, confessing that her brother died before she was born, and they never told her.

Melvin Morse is the best-known researcher in children's near-death experiences, having practiced his entire professional career as a pediatrician. His multiple books contain the kind of child-NDE case studies that continue to baffle health professionals just as adult NDEs do, but often with insights from children that are far beyond even adults' abilities to express.

The International Association for Near-Death Studies says, "Our research so far indicates that *about 85% of children who experience cardiac arrest have an NDE.* With improving cardiac resuscitation techniques, more and more children are surviving cardiac arrest. More children who have had NDEs are alive today, and the number is likely to increase because of improved resuscitative techniques. Apparently, youngsters of any age can have an NDE. Very young children, as soon as they are able to speak, have reported NDEs they had as infants or even in the process of being born."

The fact that the number of children who have NDEs is more than four times the number of adults who do, when both have had cardiac arrests, seems to suggest that adults may have developed some sort of mental deterrent. Or perhaps children who experience NDEs simply had retained a mystical relationship with their souls, which adults have lost through the "veil of forgetfulness."

Regarding children's near-death experiences, Kenneth Ring added, "These children's stories seem to be describing something that is *intrinsic* to the human personality once it is caused to enter the state of consciousness that ensues on coming close to death." Ring also revealed several less-publicized changes that happen to some child NDE survivors. He said, "What seems to happen is that the NDE unleashes normally dormant potentials for *higher consciousness* and extraordinary human functioning:

- They experience states of expanded mental awareness … flooded with information;
- [It] seems to accelerate the development of … psychic sensitivities; and
- [There is] a strong connection with the development of healing gifts afterwards."

Negative Near-Death Experiences

One of the most dramatic cases of an adult life conversion by a near-death experience was that of Howard Storm, which is described in his book *My Descent Into Death: A Second Chance At Life*. Before it happened, Storm, a professor of art at Northern Kentucky University, was *not* a very pleasant man. An avowed atheist, he was hostile to every form of religion and to those who practiced it. He would often use rage to control those around him and didn't find joy in anything. He knew with certainty that the material world was all that existed and he had no faith in anything that couldn't be seen, touched, or felt. He considered all belief systems associated with religion to be fantasies.

Then, on June 1, 1985, at the age of thirty-eight, he had a near-death experience due to a perforation of his stomach. This happened while he and his wife were on an art trip to Paris with his students. He almost did not survive.

Storm's experience was, at first, horribly gruesome, which may have reflected his worst fears. Countless creatures in a fog lured him to follow them, then began jeering and clawing at him. Terrified, he agonized, "I was alone, destroyed, yet painfully alive in the revoltingly horrible place."

Then he heard a voice saying, "Pray to God." He remembered thinking, "Why? What a stupid idea … I don't believe in God … I don't pray." Yet, a second time, then a third, he heard, "Pray to God." Then, for the first time in his adult life, a very old tune from his childhood started going through his head, "Jesus loves me…" Then, "A ray of hope began to dawn in me, a belief that there was something greater out there. For the first time in my adult life, I wanted it to be true that Jesus loved me." With all the strength he had left, he yelled, "Jesus, save me!"

Then in the darkness, a pinpoint of light appeared, like a distant star. It rapidly grew brighter and brighter, headed directly for him. He recalled, "It was indescribably brilliant, it wasn't just a light. This was a living, luminous being ... surrounded by an oval of radiance."

His book described his entire experience, including his visit to Heaven and its profound impact on his life. He resigned as a professor and redirected his life by attending Union Theological Seminary. Today, he is an ordained minister, a former pastor of the Zion United Church of Christ in Cincinnati, Ohio and later a missionary to Belize. Storm's Website is http://www.howard-storm.com.

Yet, you will find in this book some instances of religions as well as skeptics that disavow near-death experiences. I leave it to you, especially after reading Storm's experience, to contemplate why that happens.

"Visiting Heaven"

The "spirit world" is described as one of "pure thought." Near-death survivors who "visit Heaven" speak of "feeling" overwhelming love and of "knowing" their place in the vastness of it all. If this were you, you also might "view" a quick panoramic replay of your life. Therein, you typically could "sense" other peoples' part in your experiences, from *their* point of view, especially if you mistreated them in any way. You should "see" deceased relatives and close friends, appearing as you *and* they appeared on earth—in perfect health! Such "reunions" might be emotional, with each "person" carrying to "Heaven" memories of experiences with one another on Earth. Remember, of course, that your life review would extend *only* to the "present" of your life on earth.

In his first book *90 Minutes in Heaven,* Baptist minister Don Piper wrote, "I felt as if I were in another dimension. Never, even in my happiest moments, had I ever felt so fully alive. I stood speechless in front of the crowd of loved ones, still trying to take in everything." Piper had been declared dead after a dump truck crushed his small car, until a passing driver found that he was still alive.

Piper emphasized, "All of the people I encountered [in Heaven] were the same age they had been the last time I had seen them—except that all the ravages of living on earth had vanished … every feature was perfect, beautiful, and wonderful to gaze at. They embraced me, and no matter which direction I looked, I saw someone I had loved or who had loved me. They surrounded me, moving around so that everyone had a chance to welcome me to Heaven."

At some time, you may "see" beautiful and expansive landscapes with buildings, trees, flowers, and the like. Remember that subjects of spiritual (i.e., life-between-lives) hypnotic regression do *not* have this boundary restriction. The possible reason for this difference might be based upon *which* event you are experiencing. During a "near-death experience," for example, everything *may* be based upon an "interruption" in your soul's *current* incarnation. To survive, you must "go back" and therefore must *not* cross the boundary. A panoramic "life review" therefore would include only the *part* of life on earth *already lived*. As the subject of a spiritual regression, however, details you access about the spirit world may come from your soul's *memory* of Heaven and therefore be unlimited.

But *none* of the thousands of subjects of spiritual (i.e., life-between-lives) hypnotic regression have *ever* claimed to have *seen* God. However, some persons in life-between-lives hypnotic regression have told of sensing a powerful force they call the "Presence," perhaps related to the Divine.

Moreover, although the millions of near-death survivors represent every country, culture, and religion in the world, most of them *never* speak of seeing a humanly venerated individual. Yet, some others seem to consider the mystical, overwhelming Light that they all encounter as representing a venerated one—apparently because it envelops them in unconditional love beyond any they ever felt on earth! In his most recent book with Paul Perry, Raymond Moody wrote, "The experience of the Light has no known origin in the brain. No researcher has ever been able to find the origin of the 'Light'."

Ancient Gnostic Christian texts discovered at Nag Hammadi reveal compelling similarities of Gnostic comparisons between life and death and modern near-death experiences. Gnostic beliefs were considered heretical, but Brian Bain at the University of British Columbia found extensive Gnostic tracts explaining what to expect when you die. Other passages make numerous references to NDE-like "experiences" that can happen in this life, most notable of which were human encounters with a Divine Light.

Psychologist Kenneth Ring believes that a near-death experience strengthens the survivor's resolve by improving his or her conviction of self-worth. Moreover, he or she returns with a full realization of having *lost touch* with God and God's unconditional love.

But Heaven Is Far Different

But certain human religious beliefs now seem to empower some groups with a willingness *to die* for promised heavenly rewards. It therefore seems worthwhile to understand the nature of Heaven as "seen" by those who have experienced *either* near-death sudden cardiac arrest or a spiritual hypnotic regression. In sharp contrast to receiving anticipated sensual earthly pleasures or unique authority there, Heaven and its soul inhabitants seem to reflect genuine love, peace, equality, honesty, and harmony. Moreover, souls in Heaven are neither male nor female, but may incarnate into male or female bodies on earth.

As Experientially Valid as Possible

This book therefore asks you to also honor other measures that are often applied in *traditional* scientific methods, when you evaluate reports in this book. One, the consistency of testimonies, is akin to repeatability of experimental results by researchers. Another is researcher multi-factorial analysis. For example, radiation oncologist Jeffrey Long and Paul Perry's 2011 book *Evidence of the Afterlife: The Science of Near-Death Experiences* details Long and his wife, Judy's, experiences in performing both. They collected and analyzed over 1,600 personal accounts of near-death experiences from around the world. They used a hundred-item questionnaire for each participant, designed to isolate specific elements of the experience and to flag counterfeit reports.

Another measure is observer verification of physical features reported in out-of-body testimonies. For example, there is a remarkable accuracy of patients' descriptions about the medical team's appearance, equipment used, and resuscitation procedures employed for cardiac arrest. Cardiologist Michael Sabom produced one of the most objective studies to date by comparing details from two groups of cardiac-arrest patients. One group of thirty-two experienced an OBE and "observed" resuscitation efforts being made on them by the medical team. The other group of twenty-three patients did *not* have an OBE. Both groups were asked to describe their medical team's resuscitation efforts. The OBE group was uniformly accurate, including correctly recalling readings on medical machines outside their potential line of vision. Twenty of the twenty-three patients who did *not* have an OBE were highly *inaccurate* in describing their resuscitation. This is a verifiable and potentially reproducible validation of the OBE component of the NDE.

AWARE Study

Skeptics of the out-of-body (OBE) first stage of NDEs felt that they had proved their claim when the AWARE Consciousness Research Project failed to produce highly anticipated results. It had been expected that OBE experiencers—who typically report observing resuscitation efforts from elevated positions above the medical teams' performance—would be able to identify unusual colored drawings placed face-up on shelves located near the ceilings.

Researchers were appalled at the less-than-acceptable results. But noted Dutch researcher Pim van Lommel's book *Consciousness Beyond Life: The*

Science of the Near-Death Experience helped explain the likely reason. He recognized what could have reduced cardiac arrest survivors' *ability* to recall seeing these drawings. Despite such pictures being in plain sight, these patients could have suffered from a documented condition called "*inattentional* blindness." This is the phenomenon of *not* being *aware* of something in plain sight. It literally is caused by a distraction, such as watching the hectic resuscitation efforts below *on one's own body*. For example, have you ever been *unable* to find a lost object during a frantic search, only to eventually see it right in front of you?

Viktor Frankl

Out-of-body experiences have been known for a long time. Austrian psychiatrist Viktor Frankl was one of the best-known scientists to study them many years ago. However, Frankl is better known for his 1947 book *Man's Search for Meaning,* which he drew from his and other World War II prisoners' experiences in the Theresienstadt German concentration camp.

An Interesting Suggested Conflict

The Spring 2014 *Journal of Near-Death Studies* book review of Episcopal priest John Price's 2013 book *Revealing Heaven: The Eyewitness Accounts That Changed How a Pastor Thinks About the Afterlife* is worth considering here. That review makes a notable distinction between Price's convictions about NDEs and traditional Christian dogma. Price heard many life-changing NDE testimonies, including his time as an Army chaplain, which persuaded him of their validity and the reality of life after death. Although near-death experiences reflect God's unconditional love for everyone, the reviewer reminded us that traditional Christianity compels God to condemn sinners to Hell unless they believe in Jesus' payment for their sins by His crucifixion—in other words, a God of fear rather than a God of love?

Meaning of Near-Death Experiences

By now, you have been confronted with many reports that naturally differ with traditional views about life and death. I am satisfied with my quest for answers thus far. Yet, I also look forward to my continuing efforts to further validate, so far as this becomes possible, the experiential evidence which seems to support the possible "other" reality of God, Heaven, and souls.

The next chapter therefore narrows the focus to the *activity* of our souls that seems to be responsible for its experiential manifestations.

Eight

SOUL CONSCIOUSNESS

*"The first peace is that which comes
within the souls of people when they realize
their oneness with the universe and all its powers."*

BLACK ELK
SIOUX HOLY MAN

An earlier chapter discussed the "consciousness" in the womb, as illustrated by four of Feldmar's teenage patients with "hidden memories" of their mothers' attempted abortions. This therefore provided the basis for introducing experiential evidence of the incarnated soul. Later you will read much more about the soul itself.

But we should acknowledge the attribute of the soul that enables us to portray its existence in the womb. That is what might be called "soul consciousness," since we normally attribute memories to "consciousness." As you recall, the right cerebral hemisphere also manifested a type of consciousness, even though we are *not* typically aware of its memories. Yet "soul consciousness" seems remarkably more advanced than even our "waking consciousness."

Memories From the Womb

Toward the end of the last century, fascinating details began to emerge about the life of the fetus, newborn, and young child. A pioneer in this relatively new frontier of prenatal (i.e., before birth) and perinatal (i.e., surrounding birth) psychology, psychoanalyst David Chamberlain released his earlier research experiences in his 1988 book *Babies Remember Birth: And Other Extraordinary Scientific Discoveries About the Mind and Personality of Your Newborn.*

That California psychologist began his work in prenatal and perinatal psychology in the mid-1970s. This happened primarily as a result of the many surprising yet *spontaneous* responses he heard from his adult patients in *traditional* hypnotherapy. He had *unintentionally* prompted his patients in the same manner that Weiss and Newton did during their *traditional* hypnotherapy of patients, as discussed earlier.

In an online interview with Michael Mendizza on Touch the Future blog, Chamberlain spoke about how this happened: "I didn't know that people could remember birth so I just said 'Go back to when you first felt this way' [i.e., emotional trauma]. And they would go places like birth or into the womb and this was a total revelation to me. What I realized that there was something there before the brain. It took me a while to name it but there was human awareness, a human consciousness, a human intelligence that was *not* accounted for by brain development." That revelation accompanied a 75-minute video entitled *Discovering the Mind of the Prenate.*

In a 1994 Touch the Future blog interview with Suzanne Arms, Chamberlain concluded, "It's a mystery still, but in hypnosis, in a trance state, a slightly altered state from the usual consciousness, people can do amazing things with their mind, and one of the things I found they could do is remember things that you would never expect anybody to be able to remember. I've had just a steady stream of very early memories [from these hypnotized patients], not only age one or two but [also] many, many birth memories and pre-birth memories. In my experience, it doesn't seem to make a difference. People can access any of those times equally well."

APPPAH

Prenatal and perinatal psychology is now recognized in the United States as the Association for Prenatal and Perinatal Psychology and Health (APPPAH). It has a growing membership and participation in both research and practice. It has published its own quarterly journal for twenty-seven years and hosted its Nineteenth International Congress in 2015.

However, it should be emphasized that APPPAH is dedicated to reaching out to health care practitioners. But the extraordinary nature of APPPAH discoveries is naturally so revolutionary that traditional professional attitudes and beliefs may be hard to change. Yet it must be apparent to readers of this book—who obviously are *not* intrinsically bound to years of traditionally honored academic rigor, clinical austerity, and perhaps even scientific materialism—that this remarkable organization is defining new causes, detection, and treatment approaches for heretofore unrecognized emotional trauma in the womb and surrounding birth—that could otherwise remain subconsciously active for entire lives!

This book earlier acknowledged the shock among other psychotherapists that previously untreatable physical and mental problems could be successfully addressed with protocols that bordered upon the spiritual—an academically forbidden idea! Yet, all of this seems to be in the forefront of advances calling for a new scientific paradigm that could reunite health care and spirituality!

The APPPAH Web site is http://birthpsychology.com.

"Fetal" Consciousness

Womb memories from Chamberlain's hypnotically regressed adult patients offered experiential evidence of a "consciousness" in their mothers' wombs that would seem impossible with immature fetal brains. Moreover, memories have been found even in infants of emotional trauma they experienced either in the womb or during birth.

In his 2013 book *Windows to the Womb: Revealing the Conscious Baby from Conception to Birth,* Chamberlain writes, "Hypnotherapy, primal therapy, psychedelic therapies, various combinations of bodywork with breathing and sound stimulation, sand-tray therapy, and art work have all proved useful in accessing important imprints, decisions, and memories stored in the infant mind."

In his 1988 article "The Significance of Birth Memories" in the APPPAH journal *Birth Psychology*, Chamberlain had said, "Because birth memories contain so much wisdom and caring, analytical thinking and perspective, and other manifestations of higher consciousness, they raise fundamental questions about the nature of persons."

In his most recent book, Chamberlain revealed, "While brain matter has no explanatory power for such memories or any other manifestations of intelligence, emotion, or purpose during this time period, the evidence for *consciousness* remains pervasive and continuous. Thus, with no brain matter to explain them, memories continue to form and consciousness supports the human memories found at conception, shortly after conception, and the significant stream of events well *before* conception. Even more impossible to explain are the memories 'babies' display about interactions and relationships that occur over an extended period from months to years before the conception itself."

Chamberlain also explains that a "fetus" possesses an innate mind, personal yearnings, spunk, spirit, and purpose. It can exhibit telepathy (i.e., thought communication), clairvoyance (i.e., seeing objects or events beyond the five senses), out-of-body perception, and transcendent awareness.

Examples of these traits include, but are not restricted to, the following:

- Aware of the mother's, father's, or sibling's attitude about the pregnancy or toward the fetus.
- Sense imminent danger for the mother or fetus, such as umbilical cord caught around the neck, and even warn the mother psychically.
- Realize any consideration of its being aborted.
- Traumatized emotionally by maternal environment, such as loud noises or fire.
- Hostile toward the birth mother for being given away for adoption.

Naturally you wonder how these manifestations of fetal consciousness could possibly be true—such claims probably seem incredible. Yet they fit the criteria described earlier for "experiential evidence." One is from testimonies of individuals hypnotically regressed back into their mothers' wombs. Another is from traumatic fetal memories uncovered after birth in early years, typically through the various tools of child psychotherapy that Chamberlain mentioned previously.

Chamberlain cited the unusual situation involving Canadian psychologist Andrew Feldmar that you read earlier, involving the four teenage boys. Apparently without knowing about fetal consciousness at that time but with extraordinary insight, Feldmar solved their repeated suicide attempts. This appeared in Chamberlain's article "The Expanding Boundaries of Memory" in *Birth Psychology*.

Incarnated Soul?

The manifestation of such an advanced "consciousness" in the womb was as shocking to Chamberlain as past-life memory was to Weiss and life-between-lives memory was to Newton. Medical science would acknowledge that the immature fetal brain is *not* capable of this. So the actual source becomes the greater question: Is "fetal consciousness" *actually* the consciousness of the incarnated soul? Remember that Chamberlain elicited memories that reached back to *before conception*.

Chamberlain's intriguing 2012 online article "One Well-Hidden Secret of Good Parenting" paints the picture of "a [typical] prenate with at least a dozen senses, keen awareness of pain and danger, actively reaching out to communicate, and finding it difficult to cope with unloving events like neglect and silence."

Realities of Consciousness in the Womb

This section title is also the title of a chapter in David Chamberlain's book *Windows to the Womb: Revealing the Conscious Baby from Conception to Birth*. That book shatters medicine's historic view of pregnancy as a time of "infantile amnesia." But it likely still confronts a disbelieving public—and maybe even some skeptical clinicians and academicians.

Yet, apparently nobody asked the mothers-to-be themselves. Their anec-dotes are increasingly being heard as they lose fear of being considered weird for having personal experiences of "communicating" with their *unborn* chil-dren. Chamberlain acknowledges, "[Expectant] mothers who commune most with their infants know that the baby is a person, a mind and soul with un-derstanding, sensitivity, and purpose." That chapter is filled with case studies during pregnancy.

Soul and Right Hemisphere

Remember Allan Schore's emphasis on the right cerebral hemisphere's signif-icance in bonding and attachment: "The maturation of these adaptive right brain regulatory capacities is experience dependent, and this experience is embedded in the attachment relationship between the infant and primary caregiver." Further, "It is the right hemisphere and its implicit homeostatic-survival and affect regulation functions that are truly dominant in human existence."

This role of the earlier maturing right hemisphere, its increasing value in psychotherapy for "hidden memories," and its apparent accessibility for "soul consciousness" in cardiac arrest *and* soul memories through hypnotic regression—all suggest an intimate relationship between the soul and the right cerebral hemisphere. Possible implications of this will be examined in the next chapter.

Ensoulment

Chamberlain's 2013 book has an Appendix II entitled "Ensoulment: A Multicultural Synopsis." It contains these two excerpts:

- "Humans vary in our understanding as to how we become ensouled. Unfortunately few of us are willing to examine evidence that challeng-es our assumptions, causing a stalemate between materialists and spir-itualists. Many people who consider themselves 'scientific thinkers' assume there is no ensoulment at all since they believe humans and other living beings are material beings only."

- "While different religions, traditions, and teachings seem to be in conflict with each other, the great mystics of all religions, traditions, and teachings are in agreement with each other. Of course everything is conscious since God is conscious and everything that is reflects God. Each of us is a part of a great Whole."

In the following reports from other researchers, please note that a "non-visceral" entity also was sensed in the womb *separate* from the fetus. This seems to suggest the presence of two separate "identities" in the womb early in pregnancy.

From Other Researchers

Psychoanalyst Helen Wambach embarked upon research in the nineteen seventies to find answers beyond her private practice and teaching. In 1979, she released her first report in her book *Life Before Life*. This covered seven hundred and fifty adult subjects she had hypnotized into their mothers' wombs. The majority described their womb experiences as containing two "separate and simultaneous sources of awareness."

Those individuals described a "transcendent voice [that] tended to be devoid of emotion and characterize itself as a disembodied mind hovering around the fetus and mother, being in and out of the fetus. The other vantage point they reported was from the fetal human body, a perspective that was characteristically more visceral and filled with strong emotions."

Thousands of other patients who have since been hypnotically regressed into their mothers' wombs reported similar observations there. They too reported two distinct sensibilities—one was a wet, cramped somatic (i.e., body) feeling and the other was an advanced awareness, intelligence, or "consciousness" far beyond the capability of the immature fetal brain.

In APPPAH-member Wendy Anne McCarty's 2009 book *Welcoming Consciousness: Supporting Babies' Wholeness from the Beginning of Life* she expands on "fetal consciousness" with an unusual personal claim. She writes, "Underlying all of my experiences, I found I had a clear sense of myself. Often I was in the midst of a viscerally intense experience, yet I also had a *witness self* that was experiencing it from a much broader perspective. I never experienced an interruption of my sense of self."

This could mean that her "witness self" was what our book refers to as "soul consciousness" and her "visceral" experience was her somatic fetal sensation. McCarty believes that *"our primary nature is as conscious, sentient, non-physical beings that exist prior to and beyond physical human existence."*

Transcendent Source of Consciousness

Researcher Jenny Wade's article "Physically Transcendent Awareness: A Comparison of the Phenomenology of Consciousness Before Birth and After Death" appeared in a 1998 issue of the *Journal of Near-Death Studies*. In it she acknowledges that our typical understanding of consciousness is *"a brain-based source of awareness which gives us our everyday experience of the world."* But she believes that *"consciousness"* also can provide *"a physically transcendent source of awareness"* which *"predates physical life and survives bodily death."* She calls this additional state the "transcendent source of consciousness" (TSC).

Wade does not use the term "soul" for her "transcendent source of consciousness." However, footnotes in her 1996 book *Changes of Mind* do acknowledge her reluctance to use the word "soul" because she feels that it is "not sufficiently academic."

Wade emphasizes that TSC is "particularly likely to be prominent in prenatal and near-death experiences, as well as in mystical states of consciousness, but this tends to be damped out by brain-based consciousness [i.e., ego] during most of the [human] life span." She says that TSC "is pre-existent [to human life] and, as it were, 'attaches itself' in an individualized form [i.e., with the body] during the course of human life." Wade insists that human beings enter this world "wired with a dualistic spatiotemporal orientation" which enables them to "realize through spiritual practice or some other way" how to access their transcendent source of consciousness.

Incarnated But Independent

If incarnated souls *do* exist in the womb, as new experiential evidence suggests, they might be expected to be *independent* of our material bodies and therefore possibly have an *outside* source of energy. This would mean that OBEs and NDEs could occur in the shutdown of brain, heart, and lungs, as they do, and souls survive our mortal deaths.

This seems to be the conclusion of the one researcher who should know, Wilder Penfield. He was the legendary twentieth century Canadian neurosurgeon who pioneered neuropsychological studies on awake patients during brain surgery. (The brain does not have pain-sensing fibers.) His technique allowed him to create maps, still in use today, of sensory and motor cortices of the brain, showing their connections to the various limbs and organs of the body.

His experiences with the mind persuaded him to switch from materialism to dualism (i.e., reality consisting of matter *and* mind) in his continuing search for a scientific basis for the soul. He most forcefully expressed this in his final book *Mystery of the Mind: A Critical Study of Consciousness and the Human Brain:*

> "It is clear that, in order to survive death, the mind [i.e., soul] must establish a connection with a source of energy other than that of the brain. If during life (as some people claim) direct communication is sometimes established with the minds of other men or with the mind of God, then it is clear that energy from without can reach a man's mind. In that case, it is not unreasonable for him to hope that after death the mind may waken to another source of energy."

Union of Soul and Host

Michael Newton's ten years of research with life-between-lives spiritual regression concluded that the soul joins its host in the womb and the two apparently form a "relationship" that eventually shapes a single "personality" for the host. It seems intriguing to consider how a single "personality" might result.

"Personality" is a totality of characteristics that form the outer "self." As such, it reflects the individual's "waking" consciousness—his or her response to how he or she perceives the world, others, and him- or herself—as well as his or her unconscious influences.

Initially, the process of soul incarnation seems almost impossible to comprehend. Therefore the soul's incarnated presence still is considered an actuality primarily by the experiential evidence of its effects. It is important to keep in mind, however, that the soul is non-material (i.e., spirit or energy). Any "unification" of the soul-consciousness with the "waking" consciousness therefore might be non-material too, considering that science still *cannot* explain what "waking" consciousness really is.

In Newton's book for mental health professionals *Life Between Lives: Hypnotherapy for Spiritual Regression,* he explains that soul incarnation is "a slow, delicate process of incredible subtlety ... begins gently, carefully following the neurotransmitters of the [fetus's] brain while matching [the soul's] own energy vibrations with the mind of the baby."

Newton acknowledges being benefited by having "medical doctors and physiologists" among his patients and clients. He adds, "Posthypnotic suggestions have enabled [hypnotized] subjects in these professions to sketch out simplified diagrams [afterwards] of what they were trying to say about these linkages while under hypnosis."

In that book, Newton writes "Each soul has a unique immortal character ... [which] is melded with the emotional temperament, or human ego ... to produce a single but temporary personality for one lifetime. This is what is meant by the duality of our mind. With this union we are one person dealing with two internal ego (i.e., soul and human) forces inside us during life."

Soul Influence on Human Decisions

Since we are *not* aware of our souls, you may wonder how our souls could influence our personal decisions and behavior *without* our realizing it. Perhaps it is somewhat analogous to our "autonomic" nervous system (ANS) that controls our heart and respiratory rates and visceral functions. Like our soul consciousness, our ANS is always "on" yet we are *not* aware of it. But the ANS is involuntary while our soul consciousness apparently is not. Furthermore, remember that the right cerebral hemisphere creates memories that remain hidden and yet can influence us the rest of our lives.

The examples come to mind that, despite extensive malevolence in the world, some people *do* manifest empathy, compassion, and benevolence for others in times of great calamities. Newton seems to acknowledge this in writing: "While soul memory may be hidden from the level of conscious awareness through amnesia [i.e., veil of forgetfulness], thought patterns of the soul influence the human brain to induce motivations for certain actions."

One of the primary considerations is whether the soul and its host are well matched. In a later part of this book you will read that, before incarnating, each soul has the opportunity to choose its new host's family and circumstances into which to be born. Spirit world counselors are said to assist souls in their choices, which likely may involve specific challenges for further spiritual growth.

In Newton's book for mental health professionals he also says: "The choice of a particular body is intended to combine a soul's character defects and strengths with certain strong and weak human emotional temperaments to produce specific trait combinations for mutual benefits." In the later chapter on souls you will discover how varied souls' innate character can be. Yet each may also acquire character modifications shaped over many lifetimes on earth.

Obviously, such lifetime planning by souls has a long time to go astray on earth. Remember that parental and other influences in early life shape subconscious memories that can affect human behavior without our awareness of the cause. Moreover, powerful instinctive human needs and desires might energetically outweigh the soul's efforts and abilities. Furthermore, unforeseen human genetic or organic mental disorders may complicate soul-body cooperation. Also, souls may succumb to human behavior that attracts a soul's weaknesses. Hopefully, none of these or other extremes will complicate our soul's presence in our lives.

Yet, as Newton comments: "It has been said that we are never given more in life than we can handle, and to a large extent this seems to be accurate. We are who we are by design." Some readers might disagree with the first sentence of this quote. Nevertheless, reading the book, Yahuda Berg's *God Does Not Create Miracles—You Do!* might offer some help in understanding and achieving one's potential.

Later in this book you will find that each of us also may receive—but not recognize—subtle messages from our soul's psychic capabilities. Examples might include knowing who is calling when the phone rings or sensing that a distant loved one was injured. You may have experienced or at least heard of something similar, called "hunches," "gut feelings," or "intuition." But soul messages may have different characteristics from those, since souls have a psychic perspective to which we *normally* do not have access.

Evidence in the Womb

Consider, for example, accounts in the Christian New Testament about the fetus' "awareness" at a time when its brain had not yet fully developed, which was perhaps attributable to its soul. This conceivably might help explain the Christian biblical account of the yet-to-be-born John the Baptist jumping for joy in Elisabeth's womb when Mary, Jesus' mother-to-be, visited her, as is told in the Christian New Testament Gospel of St. Luke 1:41. You read that fetuses have some sort of communication bond with their mothers, perhaps through their souls. Witness St. Luke's account of Elisabeth being filled with the Holy Spirit during that visit.

The following real-life story illustrates the seeming veracity of in utero testimonies from being hypnotically regressed into the mother's womb. A woman hypnotically regressed in that manner recalled a conversation her mother-to-be had with an aunt. The fetus heard her mother-to-be say she "feared that she wouldn't see her daughter grow up." The aunt and the expectant mother were "sitting at the kitchen table, having cookies and tea." The new mother did die a short time later. Her adult daughter was curious, never having heard such a story, so she telephoned her aunt some distance away. After the woman told her aunt all the details, there was a gasp on the aunt's end of the line, and soon the incredulous question, "How could you possibly have *known* that?"

The awareness of events *outside* the womb in those examples seems to exemplify the advanced ability that Chamberlain called "fetal consciousness." From Chamberlain's and others' research, the discovery called "fetal consciousness" seems to possess abilities that equal or perhaps exceed even those extraordinary mental feats that sometimes are attributed to the human brain. In the absence of a more satisfactory explanation, might "fetal consciousness" actually be "soul consciousness"?

Further evidence of soul consciousness in the womb was included in David Chamberlain's 2003 article "The Fetal Senses: Twelve, Not Five: A New Proposal" in the APPPAH journal *Birth Psychology:*

- Although prenates have never been acknowledged for their psychic senses, they do demonstrate at least clairvoyance and telepathic sensing and attunement with parents whether they are near or far from each other; they know whether they are wanted or not; and they discern the emotional disposition and character of those around them.
- Finally, prenates also demonstrate transcendent sensing as they report out-of-body and near-death experiences. When out-of-body, for example, *no* senses should work for either babies or adults, but they do. In transcendent states, even immature senses function well and events are stored in memory—as can be demonstrated years later.

Based upon what you have read, the *possible* identification of our soul's activity as a "consciousness" seems to facilitate a new hypothesis for the *origin* of our waking consciousness, since science still is unable to explain it. This is suggested in the following chapter. Consider too that *if* this is true, the hypothesis also *might* help explain Michael Newton's earlier conclusion, "the soul joins its host in the womb and the two apparently form a 'relationship' that eventually shapes a single 'personality' for the host."

Nine

ORIGIN OF WAKING CONSCIOUSNESS

*"One does not discover new lands
without consenting to lose sight of the shore for a very long time."*

ANDRE GIDE

This chapter builds upon what you read earlier in this book, acknowledging the nature of our familiar "waking consciousness" and of the "soul consciousness" which seems manifested in the womb. As you recall, Michael Newton concluded that the soul joins its host in the womb and the two apparently form a "relationship" that eventually shapes a single "personality" for the host.

Remember, too, that "waking consciousness"—which also might be involved in developing that "personality"—is not manifested until two to three years of age, when the left cerebral hemisphere becomes active. By that time, of course, that child has imprinted emotionally charged *unconscious* memories with the help of his or her earlier-maturing right cerebral hemisphere.

However, it is also important to acknowledge here that some readers might arguably disagree with the preceding paragraph. You or others may claim that children sometimes *seem* to display "waking consciousness" much earlier. Without disagreeing with anyone, it is worthwhile to admit that this period of child development poses a fundamental issue in psychology. This involves what Emory University's Philippe Rochat addresses in his scholarly paper, "Five levels of self-awareness as they unfold early in life." It is available online. Basically, however, he writes that all parents typically notice an important change around two years of age when children begin to show "self-consciousness."

This suggests that the host's single "personality" or "self" does not become evident until *at least* two years of age. This is supported by the fact that babies do not recognize themselves in a mirror (i.e., no self-awareness) until around two years of age, according to repeated psychological studies. Any smiles when they look into a mirror much earlier have been shown to happen because they consider the reflection to be another baby.

Moreover, since science cannot explain the source of the most basic characteristic of our "waking" consciousness—what makes *you you*—this opens the door for a *new* hypothesis. Does our "waking consciousness" *independently* take shape as a result of brain-based abilities that arrive around ages two to three? Or does it result from *adaptation* of the already present "soul-consciousness" to life on earth as left-hemisphere brain faculties become active?

The "adaptation" hypothesis seems to be supported by the apparent ability of some children to recall their "past lives" (i.e., soul's previous incarnation). This starts about two to three years of age according to Jim Tucker's review paper "Children's Reports of Past-Life Memories." Enough cases have been found where details provided by the child actually match a particular deceased individual. Such findings suggest the existence of soul consciousness at two to three years of age, since it is the *only* source of past life memories.

Remember that Anthony Cicoria's "ball of energy and thought" (i.e., his soul) seemed to retain his "waking consciousness" when both left his body lying on the ground? Also consider that, although his left cerebral hemisphere that *facilitated* his "waking consciousness" was "material," so far as science can determine his "waking consciousness" could be "immaterial."

Consider too that each soul has its own *unique, eternal* identity established by the Divinity in Its creation of souls. Moreover, Chamberlain found that each fetus "possessed a sense of self [and] an interest in relationships." Could our *felt* individual identity (i.e., "me me") actually be our soul identity, although never recognized as such because we are unaware of our souls.

This idea is noteworthy in Chamberlain's 2012 online article "One Well-Hidden Secret of Good Parenting" in how he defines the nature of fetal "consciousness." He writes, "[Fetal] consciousness reflects an innate and permanent endowment of intelligent awareness that has a meaning similar to the word 'soul.' Thus, consciousness (not brain matter) is our core identity rising above particular ages or stages of physical, emotional, and mental development."

However, before you immediately reject the idea that our everyday consciousness emerges from our soul consciousness, consider what science says online about our "waking consciousness." The second through fourth points below are from Princeton University's online paper "The Universal Consciousness and the Uniqueness of the Self":

- The New York Academy of Science made a profound claim in an announcement of a 2012-13 guest lecture program "The Emerging Science of Consciousness: Mind, Brain, and the Human Experience." It said, "The complexity of the human brain and how it gives rise to our understanding and experience of the world around us [i.e., waking consciousness] is one of the greatest mysteries in science today. While recent discoveries in neuroscience are providing us with new insights into the workings of the brain, a comprehensive science of the mind is only just beginning to emerge."
- Nobel Laureate and Australian neurophysiologist Sir John Eccles claimed, "The odds are 10 to the power 10,000 against the uniqueness of the individual self [i.e., waking consciousness] being derived from the genetic uniqueness that built the associated brain. The uniqueness of the individual self must therefore arise from some external source."

- "According to David Hodgson, it [i.e., consciousness] is a fraction of the Universal Consciousness temporarily sequestered to be associated with an individual brain and perhaps scheduled to rejoin the Universal Consciousness at the moment of brain death. [This] might be regarded as a form of immortality, albeit not individual immortality."
- "The argument to be made in favor of David Hodgson's postulation of a Consciousness permeating the cosmos and existing independently of a material foundation is strong."
- The nineteenth century psychologist whom many consider a genius, F. W. H. Myers, wrote "the subliminal [i.e., subconscious] is the source of supernormal phenomena, that it functions in ways beyond the competence of the everyday self and previously unknown to science" and "this reveals the human psyche has roots in a deeper part of reality that somehow transcends space and time."

If "soul consciousness" actually is the origin of our "waking consciousness," then "soul consciousness" may serve the needs of the fetus, infant, and child for his or her first two to three years. Once the child is that age and older, his or her left cerebral hemisphere develops, cognition and ego begin, instincts kick in, conscious memories occur, and "waking consciousness" takes shape.

Soul consciousness may then remain part of our "waking consciousness," typically subject to cerebral hemisphere control, but lost to our conscious awareness because of the "veil of forgetfulness." However, remember Michael Newton's earlier claim: "While soul memory may be hidden from the level of conscious awareness through amnesia [i.e., veil of forgetfulness], thought patterns of the soul influence the human brain to induce motivations for certain actions."

Of course, the "veil" may just be perpetuated by the overwhelming nature of left-hemisphere-dominated influences. Yet consider that cardiac arrest (i.e., heart, lung, and brain death) does not affect soul consciousness, which still allows those patients to "visit Heaven." Consider too that all of these survivors describe their Heavenly visits by using the grammatical first person "I."

Consider, if you will, how well Anthony Cicoria's experience illustrates what you have read in this chapter:

- "I ... was just a ball of energy and thought."
- "... I was thinking normal thoughts."
- "I ... was capable of thought and reason."
- "This cosmic realization of consciousness meant that my self-awareness was no longer in the lifeless body on the ground."

Personal Commentary

The most recent outcome of my search were my discovery of Anthony Cicoria's detailed report of his out-of-body experience and the kind permission from the Missouri State Medical Association to reproduce it in this book. Yet he had that experience *back in 1994.* Perhaps I'm not a very good researcher.... Remember, of course, that Tony Cicoria's fame from his out-of-body experience actually lies in his marvelous newfound passion and skill in piano music.

Soul Influences

Two characteristics of the *soul* also can affect the first few years of childhood—the soul's personality and maturity. Souls have different personalities, as do humans. Soul personality and human temperament depend upon meshing with one another in order to develop a uniform personality.

Also, individual souls are at different degrees of spiritual development, learning to master human frailties. From Michael Newton's more than 7,000 case studies, he differentiated souls' progress from levels I through VI. He indicated that souls of his patients and clients typically are on the lower levels. Those on upper levels apparently have less need to continue incarnating.

Some souls, especially the less mature ones, may therefore become engrossed with their human hosts' life styles, instinctive drives, and emotions.

This might interfere with the soul's spiritual growth and require additional incarnations for specific human frailties. However, psychiatrist Joel Whitton said that souls typically leave behind any animal instincts affecting them when they depart the human body: "anger, sensual pleasure, and lust."

Support From Child Development

Kendra Cherry's online "Cognitive Development in Early Childhood" supports the idea that, at least *before age two*, children's "knowledge of the world is limited to his or her sensory perceptions, and motor activities [and] behaviors are limited to simple motor responses caused by sensory stimuli." This is based upon the work of the eminent Swiss developmental psychologist Jean Piaget. He termed the period between birth and two as the "sensorimotor stage" of infant development.

But any such talents babies seem to have before their brain faculties develop might be attributed to their soul consciousness. In early years, kids may even volunteer "psychic" remarks, such as premonitions or past-life memories.

As these children grow older, however, cares of the world will overshadow their "psychic" ability. Later in their lives, they will even disavow ever having made such remarks. This would be expected, since children's memories of experiences before age three typically are called "unconscious," "subconscious," or "implicit."

This epiphenomenon provides experiential evidence that soul consciousness exists in very young children. It also suggests that soul consciousness remains an unrecognized part of our waking consciousness.

But Kids Are Kids

Chamberlain and other APPPAH researchers found that young kids were capable of remembering their fetal and birth experiences. Before kids begin to speak, however, their complaints apparently must be "read" from their nonverbal behavior, with the help of trained counselors.

Keep in mind the constellation of events and emotions that are *subconsciously* recorded during those first years! Imagine what a shock being born must be—to souls as well as to babies—plus the many other earthly experiences that follow for the next couple of years! It therefore seems natural that "soul" consciousness focuses primarily on being a kid, adjusting to the new life and the many human influences to which it is exposed.

But don't expect soul consciousness to make kids "little angels." Remember that these are "little humans," and all their present experiences are in a human environment. What's more, everyone treats them as babies, then children. If they do shock you with a premonition, for example, they didn't think it was strange—unless you sharply reacted.

In other words, they are more human than spirit beings, and we typically treat them that way. Soul consciousness seems to simply facilitate their growing awareness and improving perceptiveness. As brain faculties come online, they may just complement soul consciousness.

Just as the "scientific method" can never be used to validate the reality of near-death experiences, it can't be used to verify that the brain alone is responsible for "waking" consciousness. The brain can never be isolated from the soul.

Veil of Forgetfulness

But, if our everyday consciousness did develop from soul consciousness, you might ask why our souls can't control human behavior, to keep us from pursuing self-gratification, wealth, and power? There seem to be two possible reasons. One is inherent in how our brain operates, as you read earlier—our souls may have to compete with stronger instinct and ego forces acting through the "dominant" left cerebral hemisphere.

The other reason seems to be the result of the legendary "veil of forgetfulness," with its historic philosophical and theological background. This blocks our conscious awareness of our souls *and* any lessons they learned during previous incarnations. Witness the need for hypnotic regression to access soul memories. The online "Teachings Concerning the Veil of Forgetfulness" collected by B. Satterfield offers spiritual commentaries.

This overall concept is naturally mind-boggling! But science knows little about how our waking consciousness exists or operates. So please withhold your possible incredulity, to fully contemplate the implications for each of us and our loved ones.

The next chapter suggests the nature of "The *Real* You" as is intended in this book's title. But you will have to wait until later chapters to explore more about your soul, its reincarnation, and its immortality, as well as the eternal system of checks and balances in soul self-accountability called "karma"—all of which will involve your soul "Whether You Like It or Not."

Ten

THE *REAL* YOU

*"Most people live, whether physically, intellectually, or morally,
in a very restricted circle of their potential being.
They make very small use of their possible consciousness
and of their soul's resources in general."*

WILLIAM JAMES

B efore you decided to read this book, you may have felt that you knew the *real* you. Maybe you were very comfortable, even smug, about it. As you will see in the final chapter, each of us passes through multiple stages of life. We are influenced in different ways by an expanding number of people. Depending upon how we feel about ourselves, we may make adjustments in our behaviors and allegiance. We likely will be concerned about impressions that others have *of us*. Sometimes this may lead us to develop a façade that we even may believe is "the *real* you."

But this book reaches beyond that, to an inner self of which you were never aware. It is your God-given soul—each human being has one. Souls have sometimes been called "sparks of God." That seems to mean that our souls were created for us by God to have special knowledge and capabilities that would enable them to be *our* direct links with the Almighty and the spirit world. Your soul's *immortal* identity therefore distinguishes it from every other soul and gives it that same exclusive identity in every host in which your soul ever has or will incarnate.

Discerning "The Real You"

Anthony Cicoria's revealing out-of-body experience illustrated that he was totally *unaware* that his "ball of energy and thought" was his soul. It seems likely that he was not familiar with the concept, perhaps the result of the "veil of forgetfulness." Yet he knew something was very different when his legs vanished and he simply passed through the wall. Also, he knew that "he" was invisible! What if that had been you, especially if you had *already* read this book?

Naturally, most sudden cardiac arrest victims are shocked to find "themselves" floating in an upper corner of the room, "watching" hectic resuscitation efforts on their body on a gurney below, by a trauma medical team! However, there is a near-unbelievable account from Mellen-Thomas Benedict who, in 1982, is said to have miraculously returned to his body after an hour and a half when monitors showed no vital signs. But he apparently also had received a complete remission of his earlier terminal illness! Yet the other fantastic part of his experience was what he was able to learn *and* his subsequent continuing ability to access to what he calls "Universal Intelligence." Obviously, my book can take no position on this account but, if true, it provides me with a lead for my continuing quest, whose potential implications seem unlimited about the "spirit world." Yet you can investigate this for yourself at his new Website (http://mellen-thomas.com).

Many millions of near-death survivors now live around the world. Most probably have not been introduced to what you find in this book. Yet, if they experienced the second stage, "visiting Heaven" apparently was enough for them to come back convinced of most of what you read in this book.

Obviously, scientists continue to propose theories to try to explain your "waking" consciousness. But only the kind of research that involves *material* reality is tolerated in academia and in peer-reviewed professional journals.

So the previous chapter in this book suggested that the *origin* of your "waking" consciousness is our *non-material soul consciousness* that incarnated in the womb. Thereafter, during birth and the first two to three years, it may have served your early needs, but deprived you of soul memories by the "veil of forgetfulness." Eventually, your soul consciousness adapted to living on earth through cognitive faculties from your left hemisphere to create your "waking" consciousness.

Naturally, Anthony Cicoria's detailed account of his out-of-body experience from his sudden cardiac arrest revealed his apparently authentic recollections, including:

- "I had lost all form entirely and instead was just a ball of energy and thought."
- "It suddenly occurred to me that I was thinking normal thoughts."
- "I, whatever I was now, was capable of thought and reason."
- "The people around my body could not see or hear me."
- "But I could see and hear everything they did and said."
- "This cosmic realization of consciousness meant that my self-awareness was no longer in the lifeless body on the ground."

Remember, too, that researcher Michael Newton commented earlier in this book:

"Each soul has a unique immortal character ... [which] is melded with the emotional temperament, or human ego ... to produce a single but temporary personality for one lifetime. This is what is meant by the duality of our mind. With this union we are one person dealing with two internal ego (i.e., soul and human) forces inside us during life."

Never Before Known

Some findings in Sam Parnia's book *Erasing Death: The Science That Is Rewriting the Boundaries Between Life and Death* seem pertinent here. He wrote, "That entity that we define as consciousness, the soul, or the self—that which makes me who I am—does not stop existing just because someone has entered the period beyond death." But he *also* said, "To better explain the scientific situation we find ourselves in [i.e., 'near-death' survival], it is as if we have discovered a wholly new type of substance that we can neither account for nor even explain in terms of anything we have ever seen and dealt with before in science." That seems to help reinforce this book's contention that "the *real* you" is immortal.

"Conscious" Decisions?

Incredibly, neuroscience has now proved that at least some so-called "conscious decisions" may be made *unconsciously*, several seconds before we are *aware* of them. One source of such evidence is the Max Planck Institute for Human Cognitive and Brain Sciences in Leipzig, Germany. Yet similar proof also comes from studies elsewhere. Professor Marcus Du Sautoy's online article about this is entitled "Brain Scans Can Reveal Your Decisions 7 Seconds Before You 'Decide'."

The "Mind"

Almost any dictionary you might consult will define "mind" as what you read earlier for "waking consciousness." So this leads to what is called the "mind-body problem." Eminent philosopher Thomas Nagel expressed it this way: "The mind-body problem exists because we naturally want to include the mental life of conscious organisms in a comprehensive scientific understanding of the world. On the one hand it seems obvious that everything that happens in the mind depends on, or is, something that happens in the brain. On the other hand the defining features of mental states and events, features like their intentionality, their subjectivity, and their conscious experiential quality, seem *not* to be comprehensible simply in terms of the physical operation of the organism."

You may agree with Nagel that your experiences with "waking" consciousness occasionally create within you personal feelings of "intentionality" and "subjectivity" with regard to certain matters. For example, these could involve decisions that you alone can make, different from usual "waking" consciousness responses to external events.

Historical Significance of the Right Hemisphere

Probably the most respected psychologist, researcher, and scholar in the historical underpinnings of the significance of the right cerebral hemisphere was the late Julian Jaynes. The following is reproduced from his paper "Consciousness and the Voices of the Mind" at the 1983 McMaster-Bauer Symposium on Consciousness, with the kind permission of the Julian Jaynes Society, Henderson, NV:

> "At the time that I was thinking in this primitive fashion [i.e., bicameral mind], in the early 1960s, there was little interest in the right hemisphere. Even as late as 1964, some leading neuroscientists were saying that the right hemisphere did nothing, suggesting it was like a spare tire. But since then we have seen an explosion of findings about right hemisphere function, leading, I am afraid, to a population that verges on some of the shrill excesses of similar discussions of asymmetrical hemisphere function in the latter part of the 19th century and also in the 20th century."
>
> "What I have tried to present to you is a long and complicated story. It leaves us with a different view of human nature. It suggests that what civilized us all is a mentality that we no longer have, in which we heard voices called gods. Remnants of this are all around us in our own lives, in our present-day religions and needs for religion, in the hallucinations heard particularly in psychosis, in our search for certainty, in our problems of identity. And we are still in the arduous process of adjusting to our new mentality of consciousness. The final thought I will close with is that all of this that is most human about us, this consciousness, this artificial space we imagine in other people and in ourselves, this living within our reminiscences, plans, and imaginings, all of this is indeed only 3,000 years old."

Allan Schore wrote, "The unconscious represents the inner world described by psychoanalysis since its inception." Even though he made this claim about your "right hemisphere unconscious," it seems *not too* implausible that—since you are *not* aware of your soul, which is hypnotically accessed through your right hemisphere—a similar claim might apply to your soul too.

Subtle Body Energy

Valerie Hunt's book *Infinite Mind: Science of Human Vibrations of Consciousness* offers an aspect of the mind that still is not fully developed, despite her book's first publication in 1989. This involves what might be called the "subtle energy body." Two apparent manifestations are called "auras" and "chakras." "Auras" are said to be invisible to most people, but are described as resembling a "halo" of luminous radiation appearing in the shape of, and surrounding, a person's body. Some religious art contains them around revered figures. "Chakras" have been termed "wheels of energy" throughout the body. Claims are made that both auras and chakras reflect the state of the person's health. You likely are more familiar with the increasingly popular practices of acupuncture and yoga, both of which seem to involve such subtle body energy.

Ironically, there may be clinical and spiritual truth for claims about these concepts. For example, Chamberlain's 2013 book contained the following: "Two-to-six-year-old children who haven't been taught better nearly always draw human figures who are surrounded by colors. However, when their teachers point out that humans do not have any colors around them, the children obediently quit drawing the auras."

Notably, Constance Rodriguez authored an article in *The Llewellyn Journal* that complements this discussion. Entitled "The Subtle Energy Body: Your Passport to the Mystical Realms," it describes what is subtitled "The First Four Levels of the Subtle Body." These are called "etheric," "emotional," "mental," and "astral" bodies. Without further discussion here, these are mentioned because, although manifestations of the soul departing from the physical body at death are not consistent, any such appearance may involve "subtle energy bodies."

Religious History

As mentioned earlier, history reflects that Greek philosophers like Socrates, Aristotle, and Plato discussed souls, as did early Christian theologians like Origen. Moreover, reincarnation was a common belief in Jesus' time. However, according to Christian scholar Elizabeth Jenson, early Church Fathers who were accused of teaching reincarnation had their works banned. So it was dropped from debate at the Council of Constantinople in 553 CE. Jenson wrote, "It was believed to contradict the doctrine of corporeal resurrection and undermine the need for Christ's redemptive sacrifice."

Christianity, Judaism, and Islam are faith-based religions. Therefore all of these respect and acknowledge the actuality of the Eternal Almighty and Heaven (i.e., the "afterlife"). So it must be acknowledged that institutional religion helped over the centuries to encourage caring for one another and thereby to curb self-gratification and violence. You will find commentaries later in this book about the soul from Catholicism, Judaism, and Islam.

The Jewish heritage from which Christianity emerged reveals a historic respect for the soul. On the Web site aish.com, Rabbi Aryeh Kaplan discusses "The Soul: Understanding the Source of Our Soul and Its Eternal Essence." Of all religions, Judaism's perspective of the soul seems the most akin to what is presented in this book.

Mysticism and Enlightenment

Mysticism originated in the depths of history and has always been respected for what it is: the apparent ability of some individuals to have spiritual experiences based deep inside themselves. English author and broadcaster Karen Armstrong's book *Visions of God* reflects her prodigious effort to understand and share with others the personal religious-spiritual experience. These excerpts are from her book:

> "The actual experience of all mystics is strikingly similar. All encounter a reality in the depths of the self that is, paradoxically, Other and irrevocably separate from us. All emphasize that this ultimate reality,

which gives meaning and value to human life, is ineffable, transcending our limited words and concepts. Jewish and Muslim mystics also emphasized the transcendence of the God who would never be known by the human soul in its entirety—even in the next world. In the late twentieth century, therefore, people may find the mystical experiment, which also urges the adept to look within himself for the truth and warns against the danger of simplistic ideas and projections about God, to be a more attractive form of religion than the more conventional and dogmatic types of faith."

It may be worth recalling the other reference early in this book to mysticism, referring to the Gospel of Thomas:

"Yet Thomas takes Jesus' private teachings in a different direction from John. For example, the divine light that Jesus represents is shared by all humanity, since we all are made in the image of God. Therein, the Gospel of Thomas initiates a central theme of Jewish, and eventually Christian, mysticism a thousand years later—the "image of God" is hidden in everyone, typically without his or her awareness, but secretly linking God and all humanity."

The goal of our soul's spiritual growth is sometimes called "enlightenment." But achievement of enlightenment should *not* be viewed with any feeling of self-righteousness, as might be typical of the human ego. Rather, spiritual advancement is viewed by the soul with great humility, as is expressed in these lines from an ancient poem by a Chinese Zen master: "Before enlightenment, chop wood, carry water; after enlightenment, chop wood, carry water."

Yet our willingness to contemplate the *possible* truth of our divine nature need not seem threatening in any way. Physically, you are the same human being you were before picking up this book. Mentally, you are as secure as ever in your felt persona. Spiritually, you have added a new understanding—neither religious nor scientific dogma can inhibit your assurance that you are both human *and* spiritual.

Search for Meaning

Yet the "search for meaning" addressed in many best-selling books has more of a contemporary significance than many people may realize. More recently, the importance of such quests has been raised in two disparate scientific disciplines: *psychology* and *physics*. It therefore seems fitting to examine these too in the context of "the *real* you."

For example, Michael Price's article "Searching for Meaning" in the American Psychology Association's *Monitor on Psychology* carries this subtitle, "Existential-humanistic psychologists hope to promote the idea that therapy can change not only minds but lives." The following is quoted from that article with the APA's expressed permission:

> "What if you want answers broader than a diagnosis or a neurochemical explanation for why your brain does what it does? What if you want to know how to lead a fuller, richer life, not just change a problematic behavior? Many people want a more holistic experience that does more than address their symptoms. They want a therapy that helps them know more about their lives and feelings."

Now switch from the internal to the celestial. In an announcement of a series of programs with the New York Academy of Science, the Nour Foundation linked them with the intriguing title, "Beyond the Big Bang: Searching for Meaning in Contemporary Physics." The program description contained these words:

> "Perhaps more than any other scientific discipline, modern physics has revolutionized our understanding of the cosmos by tackling a number of age-old existential questions. For all its successes, physics has also uncovered new mysteries, from dark energy and dark matter to the perplexing properties of quantum mechanics and the possibility of multiple universes. While new discoveries have pushed us to the frontiers of science, they have also raised fundamental questions regarding what physics can ultimately reveal about the nature of our

reality. Has modern physics lost touch with our basic intellectual and existential concerns? Can physics help us to understand what it means to be human, or are we merely insignificant specks in the cosmos?"

Earth's Finality

Remember the earlier comments about the End of Days, Armageddon, and Day of Judgment? The term "apocalypse" has been collectively applied to those "end times." But its origin is the Greek word *apokalypsis*—since most early religious writings were in Greek—meaning a "revealing" or an "unveiling." The prolific author Peter Lorie pursued this in his unique analysis of St. John's biblical book in Lorie's book of the same name, *Revelation*. Lorie is better known for his books on Nostradamus.

That Christian New Testament book has remained enigmatic and troubling to theologians and religious followers alike. But Lorie offers an interpretation where joy, crisis, and self-discovery lead to a future age with a positive understanding of our world and our selves. Therefore, given the human folly rampant in today's "civilized" world, would we *not* better avoid nuclear self-destruction of Earth by acknowledging our apparent common *spiritual* heritage through our souls?

Yet, considering the dramatic expansion of the cosmos far beyond what was believed two thousand years ago—when Earth was "the center of the universe" and when the apocalypse was expected sooner than later—the only way it might happen now seems to be nuclear self-destruction rather than the biblical "Day of Judgment." Moreover, the "spirit world" and the rest of the cosmos would seem to remain untouched.

Therefore, from all you have read in this book, does *any* religion's prediction still seem possible for Earth, to include: "Day of Judgment;" "corporeal resurrection of all human bodies that ever have lived on earth;" or the "return of any revered person or soul from Heaven to conquer evil forever for that religion's followers"?

Being part of the "other" reality, souls obviously are imperceptible to human physical senses. Later chapters will be devoted to understanding souls and their immortality, as best can be gathered from references available today. Yet, remember that *experiential* evidence now exists about souls. Recall too that "fetal consciousness," near-death experiences, psychic abilities of some young children, inexplicable adult psychic experiences, and both end-of-life and shared-death experiences—all of which seem to involve souls— are acknowledged phenomena for which science has *no* indisputable explanations.

The next chapter therefore will discuss what is involved in souls "returning home" at the death of the human body, from the perspectives of a dying loved one, of his or her surviving soul, and of his or her survivors.

Eleven

Souls "Return Home"

"Death is simply a shedding of the physical body
like the butterfly shedding its cocoon. It is a transition to a
higher state of consciousness where
you continue to perceive, to understand,
to laugh, and to be able to grow."

Elisabeth Kubler-Ross

You, like me, may have a nagging feeling about never seeing your loved ones again. That is reasonable in the current societal climate of secularism and self-gratification. Even funerals and worship services today seem *unable* to rekindle faith in the afterlife, given our belief in only a common-sense reality. That is why this book—like the many others about near-death experiences—may be difficult to accept, even as *possibly* true. Maybe it all sounds too good to be true, so you are afraid to let yourself believe. Therefore, please consider what you find in *every* discussion in this book as thoughtfully as possible before drawing conclusions.

Note: this is a chapter that addresses one of the two *other* objectives of this book cited in the Introduction: "the brash *willingness* by terrorists to seek death for *false* promises of reward in Heaven."

Dying and death are being studied today with unusual interest. Even though both are still dreaded, researchers are finding that the end-of-life is not instantaneous. Nor is death simple. Perhaps the primary reason dying and death may seem more complex in this book is its acknowledgment of our souls. Scientists and health professionals may still be criticized by their peers for linking the end of life with the spiritual. However, some prominent researchers are helping to bridge the chasm. This chapter discusses dying and death from the perspective of a few of those researchers.

"Returning Home"

Hypnotically regressed patients and clients have used the term "return home" for departure of the soul after death of the physical body. When the soul returns to the spirit world after death of the body, subsequent events seem to depend on the individual soul.

Apparently, the spirit world receives returning souls in a manner which best accommodates feelings and needs of that soul; integrity of its energy state; and its need for continued spiritual growth. However, returning souls expect to have their reception conditioned to some extent by their success, or lack of it, in helping their hosts overcome human frailties.

Toronto ON psychiatrist Joel Whitton stressed that a soul's initial reaction to departing at death of the physical body usually is the same, regardless of the number of its reincarnations. Upon exiting the "tunnel," one or more souls of previously departed friends and relatives may be waiting at the "Gateway" to welcome each arriving soul. There is nothing haphazard about those friends or relatives knowing *exactly* when souls are due and where to meet them in the spirit world. This can have an overwhelming impact on many returning souls upon seeing previously departed people whom the dying *person* may have doubted *ever* seeing again.

Whitton said that souls typically leave *behind* any *animal* instincts affecting them when they depart the human body: "anger, sensual pleasure, lust, sadness, and jealousy." Newton found that "some souls do carry the negative baggage of a difficult past life longer than others." But Newton and Whitton both stressed that soul adjustment to the spirit world depends upon "the soul's level of spiritual growth; its attachment to memories left from this life on earth; and the nature and timing of death." At the Gateway to the spirit world, the baggage starts to diminish. The soul soon recognizes the "carefully directed order and harmony" of the "world" it had left for its most recent incarnation.

The soul's departure from the mortal body is sometimes unevenly timed. Much research has been done on what are called end-of-life (EOL) experiences. In September 2015, Raymond Moody inaugurated an investigation with Bryn Athyn College's Erica Goldblatt Hyatt and Lisa Smartt entitled "Research Into Communications of the Dying." This was accompanied by the live-stream panel presentation, "The Unintelligible Afterlife." You may recall that Moody was the first researcher to publicize "shared-death" experiences, during which members of the loved one's family sometimes may share in his or her soul's transition into the afterlife.

End-of-Life Research

Dying persons seem aware when death is approaching. Their comments and behavior typically are characteristic of what are now called "end-of-life" (EOL) experiences. British psychiatrist Peter Fenwick is internationally recognized for his "end-of-life" research.

One unusual kind of phenomenon seems to attest to the psychic actuality of such experiences: dying ones claim to be "visited" by previously deceased loved ones. But surprisingly, these "visitors" may include a friend or relative who died recently *without the patient's knowledge*.

Deceased "visitors" apparently offer to return closer to the time of death and even to come and escort the soul to Heaven. It has been reported that dying ones also seem able to time their departure. This might involve delay if the patient has an unsettled personal or business matter. It also might be the patient's choice to leave while family members are absent. Certain rare events also have occurred—strange animal behavior or clocks stopping—at the time of death. Remarkably, a particular cat in a northeastern medical facility became a media celebrity when staff nurses discovered that it would snuggle next to patients who soon died.

The soul and its consciousness therefore seem evident *during* its transition, too, into a different realm at death of the physical body. This seems in keeping with critical care physician Sam Parnia's claim that death is *not* an instant event. His 2013 book *Erasing Death: The Science That is Rewriting the Boundaries Between Life and Death* emphasizes, "Death is not a single point but a process."

Much of British psychiatrist Peter Fenwick's life has been devoted to studying deathbed phenomena and what these mean in the greater picture of who we *really* are. His work seems to illuminate soul consciousness and the soul's survival of mortal death. He has written several books, including *The Art of Dying, The Truth in the Light,* and *The Hidden Door.* Fenwick has developed a number of observations about dying, which he shared in a 2012 interview, "Dr. Peter Fenwick Discusses Dying, Death, and Survival" on Michael Tymn's Blog.

From among his and others' experiences involving end-of-life research, we learn of many observations about events some patients may describe or may even be witnessed by others. These include the following:

- Some people will have a premonition that they will die within two years.
- The dying will be visited by a dead relative nearer to the time of death.
- Deceased relatives and spiritual figures appear to the dying and tell them that they will be back to pick them up, and perhaps when.
- The dying may be able to negotiate postponement of their death by a little.
- The dying hover in and out of a reality that is full of love, light, spiritual beings, and deceased relatives, very much like an actual-death experience.
- Just before death, paralyzed people sometimes are able to sit up and Alzheimer's patients sometimes regain their memory for periods of time.

- The dying will sometimes visit someone to whom they are emotionally attached. Distance and time are not factors.
- The dying see a mirage, sparks, and radiant light.

Plato said, "Once free of the body, the soul is able to see truth clearly, because it is more pure than before and recalls the pure ideas which it knew before."

Peter Fenwick offered the following that seem to qualify more as after-death communications:

- Coincidences that happen around the time of death, involving the appearance of the dying person to a close relative or friend who is not physically present.
- Phenomena that occur around the time of death: such as clocks stopping, strange animal behavior, or lights and equipment turning on and off.

As you reflect on shared-death experiences and end-of-life events reflected in this chapter, remember these statements:

- Not all persons have witnessed the incredible experiences associated with a soul's departure into a different realm during death of the mortal body.
- For those who have, these represent psychic manifestations of the soul's amazing capabilities and perhaps psychic linking with witnesses' souls.
- All of these experiences certainly qualify as experiential evidence.

Maggie Callahan and Patricia Kelley, both hospice professionals, published their experiences under the endearing title, *Final Gifts: Understanding the Special Awareness, Needs, and Communications of the Dying*. This is a first-hand collection of stories worth reading about end-of-life events.

In the paper, "Deathbed Observations by Physicians and Nurses," psychologist Karlis Osis studied 640 reports from ten thousand American physicians and nurses about patients' visions as they faced death. These typically occurred in unsedated patients, whose minds were clear at the time. Their visions often had characteristics that are common to actual-death experiences. Similarly, "shared-death experiences" deal with a variety of extra senses, including telepathy, clairvoyance, and even out-of-body experiences, as mentioned earlier. Pain, experienced earlier, disappeared. Patients spoke of seeing angels, other worlds, or deceased loved ones, and they knew they were dying

For some unknown reason, however, *not* every death will offer nearby persons a shared-death experience, just as *not* all cardiac arrest victims have an actual-death experience. This seems especially true for hospice personnel, perhaps because they are involved almost exclusively with dying patients.

Shared–Death Experiences

Obviously it is easy to challenge the authenticity of NDEs by claiming that they are hallucinations (i.e., "all in the head"). After all, they do occur to individuals. But suppose you were standing with other family members around the bed of a dying relative and *all* of you were swept up in an inexplicable sensation of joining your loved one in his or her "nearing-death vision"?

During the mid-1980s, Moody began hearing an increasing number of personal reports about shared-death experiences from a variety of health care practitioners and laypersons around the world, especially during his lecture tours here and abroad. Then, in 1994, he had his own shared-death experience—actually, it included his wife, his two sisters, and their husbands—as they held hands around their mother's hospital bed. Moody wrote, "It was as though the fabric of the universe had torn and for just a moment we felt the energy of that place called Heaven."

In his and Paul Perry's book *Glimpses of Eternity: Sharing a Loved One's Passage from This Life to the Next,* Raymond Moody emphasizes his conviction that "shared-death" experiences reveal the truth of the afterlife more than actual-death experiences. The "father of the near-death [i.e., actual-death] experience" claims, "Because shared-death experiences eliminate what I call the escape clause of belief. Many people believe that a near-death [i.e., actual-death] experience is nothing but a hallucination. But doubters can't say that with a shared-death experience. Why? Because the people who report these experiences are *not* near death. Shared death experiences happen to healthy people."

Although Moody and other NDE researchers have yet to objectively demonstrate scientific proof of the near-death experience, Moody and other researchers now are collecting data for analysis from a growing number of cases of *shared*-death experiences. The University of Nevada in Las Vegas hosted a conference on these "new experiences," and Moody's book has an entire chapter on "Historic Parallels."

Moody's book also contains a chapter on "Elements of the Shared-Death Experience," which describes the following aspects that often have been reported by participants. But apparently not every element occurs in all shared-death group experiences:

- "Geometrical changes in the room's shape and a wall opening to a larger dimension;
- "Indescribable mystical and brilliant light of purity, love, and peace;
- "Music or musical sounds;
- "Out-of-body experience allowing participants to engage with the patient's departure;
- "Participation with the dying person in a panoramic review of his or her life;
- "Perception of heavenly realms of unearthly quality, serenity, purity; and
- "Mist or vaporescence over the patient's body appears in a human-like shape."

For purposes of this book, shared-death experiences do seem to contain an extra feature that may facilitate the observers' (e. g., family members') experience—*empathy*. Moody says, "A well-developed sense of empathy is one such [common] element that most of the *experiencers* seem to have. Another such element is a sense of acceptance or surrender that the loved one is going to die."

So, if we accept that the loved one's soul is being welcomed back to Heaven by the spirit world itself, and that empathy is a characteristic of the right hemisphere, then shared-death experiences seem entirely possible—given the psychic capabilities cited earlier for the souls of *both* the loved one and his or her family members.

Moody also explains, "Shared-death experiences deal with the notion of a variety of extra senses, including telepathy, clairvoyance, remote viewing, astral projection, spontaneous out-of-body experiences and perhaps others that I have not yet anticipated." In his book, readers can find examples of many of these among the varied personal accounts from around the world. Moody makes another notable claim, "I consider them [shared-death experiences] a picture window into the afterlife."

As Moody and Perry's book emphasizes, however, the shared-death experience typically enables nearby family members and professionals to share some of the dying one's experiences, including many listed earlier. Hopefully, word will spread within health care and soon to the clergy to enable those professionals to offer family members a reassurance *unlike* any other—perceived proof of the afterlife—for those fortunate enough to witness such events. If you still doubt, Moody and Perry's book is filled with first-hand reports from lay people, from various kinds of health care providers, and even from medical school professors.

After-Death Communications

These are called by many terms but involve "awareness" at some distance that a loved one has died, sometimes eerily at the moment of death. Remember the strange foreboding feeling *earlier* in this book that a loved one or close friend may have died? In his book *Lessons from the Light: What We Can Learn from the Near-Death Experience*, psychologist Kenneth Ring described these as "after-death communications" (ADCs). He said they are *"perhaps the single most relevant variety of death-related experience."*

Ring also revealed that Bill and Judy Guggenheim "personally amassed more than 3,300 accounts of [such] cases indicative of *real*—not hallucinatory—contact with deceased loved ones. They chose to present about ten percent of these, some 350 stories," in their book *Hello from Heaven: A New Field of Research After-Death Communication Confirms That Life and Love Are Eternal.*

ADCs are sometimes called grief-induced "hallucinations" by skeptics. But the Guggenheims' case studies include many persons who perceived ADCs from loved ones *before* they were otherwise notified that their loved ones had died. Kenneth Ring stressed, *"They [ADCs] seem strongly to suggest that those dear to us who have died continue to exist after death, and that they can communicate to us in ways that help to heal us of our grief and enable us to let go."*

Obviously, ADCs mean more to loved ones than to the general public. Yet books about these personal experiences may become best sellers for a time. No doubt William Peter Blatty's 2015 *Finding Peter: A True Story of the Hand of Providence and Evidence of Life After Death* will have such an attraction. It likely should when you realize that Blatty was the best-selling author and Oscar-award winning screenwriter of *The Exorcist.*

Similarly, James A. Pike's 1968 *The Other Side: An Account of My Experiences with Psychic Phenomena* launched a cascade of shock and curiosity—"shock" because the author at that time was the Episcopal Bishop of the diocese of California.

Naturally, reports of "after-death communications" might be dismissed as falsified or imagination. But several that Pike described seemed to have resulted from poltergeist activities (i.e., physical disturbances). Moreover, his colleagues and friends witnessed some of these.

It is estimated that almost one-third of Americans have experienced an "after-death communication" from a deceased loved one, according to Julie Beischel, director of research at the Windbridge Institute. These manifestations naturally have occurred in a wide variety of ways, and the survivor's realization is conditioned by his or her willingness to accept such phenomena as real. It may be nothing more than the characteristic whiff of the deceased's favorite dinner entrée late in the evening or the hallway grandfather clock stopping at the exact time of the loved one's demise. Yet, why should his or her grieving spouse deny this reminder that love reaches across all borders?

Taboos

Yet, people never discuss *their* deaths. When the topic does arise, it invariably pertains to the deaths of other people. As a result, survivors often are left to deal with legal, financial, and funeral arrangements as well as grief. Physicians and nurses used to be forbidden to even mention "death" or "dying." The subject still remains taboo in many cases, felt to represent a treatment failure.

The last two weeks of our lives has been called the "most expensive," as family members and even patients demand the most advanced and expensive procedures to delay death. One clergy member suggested that it is more humane for family members to reassure their loved ones that "It's OK to go," rather than "Hang in there!"

Yet dying is still one of our greatest fears, for our selves and for our loved ones. It always is untimely, coming as a shock or after long anxiety. Therefore, grief over the loss of a loved one is always natural—one who is very dear to our hearts, whose *earthly* presence we will see no more. No other demand on our lives seems so traumatic, with its turbulent upheaval in survivors' lives.

Recently, however, credible reports of experiential evidence from various disciplines are urging acknowledgment and research about phenomena at the opposite ends of our lives—conception and mortal death. These involve the apparent presence of the soul early in the womb and its seeming survival and passage into a new realm of existence during death of the mortal body.

New Horizon

But individualism is now challenging the status quo. More than twenty-two million patients around the world have told of "visiting Heaven" during their near-death experiences (NDEs). Individual spirituality is being encouraged, with benefits for health as well. Between NDEs and individual spirituality an unusual link exists, which just might infuse funerals with more optimism—a reassurance of reunions with loved ones in Heaven.

So consider this. Neither God nor Heaven is likely to be personally accepted as "real" by everyone until our bodies die *and* only when we experience the afterlife firsthand. Yet actual manifestations of fetus' emotional trauma, shared-death experiences, cardiac arrest survivors' testimonies, and hypnotic regression accounts—*all* offer *experiential evidence* of souls and soul consciousness:

- to document the incarnation of the soul into the womb;
- to participate with the soul's departure from the body at death;
- to preview the afterlife through near-death experiences; and
- to recall soul memories through hypnotic regression.

These details, acquired from thousands of experiences and studies, can be correlated to provide an encouraging promise of our souls' existence *and* its survival of mortal death. This offers a positive step too, toward acknowledging the also-imperceptible reality of God and Heaven.

The next chapter begins a discussion about our souls. The phenomena discussed there actually seem to be experiential evidence of our "soul consciousness".

Twelve

OUR ETERNAL SOULS

*"I simply believe that some part of the human Self
or Soul is not subject to the laws of space and time."*

CARL JUNG

Souls, like God and Heaven, obviously seem to be part of the "other" reality that is humanly imperceptible and inexplicable. That "reality" apparently stretches far beyond the current paradigm of scientific materialism. The "spiritual forces" of that expanded reality might even be cosmic and eternal. Naturally, you probably find this hard to accept or even imagine!

But the experiential evidence in this book could be hard to dispute—that our souls incarnate in the womb and move from our expiring physical body back into the apparently eternal realm of the afterlife in Heaven. If this is true, it also seems increasingly difficult for anyone to *deny* that souls and Heaven both are part of an expanded reality of the Divine. Still, however, I suspect that all of this will forever be beyond the reach of human science to prove *or* disprove. It would then remain an everlasting mystery of life.

Note: this is a chapter that addresses one of the two *other* objectives of this book cited in the Introduction: "the brash *willingness* by terrorists to seek death for *false* promises of reward in Heaven."

The idea that you have a soul may surprise you, especially if you seldom, if ever, heard the term "soul" mentioned. Even if you are a "religious" person, you certainly *never* heard it explained. Undoubtedly, you never understood that it has such an intrinsic role in your earthly life. But consider from the discussion on soul consciousness that our souls were created by the Divine Source to exemplify Its wisdom and power as well as Its unconditional love for each and every one of us.

Notice my use of the term "It" for the eternal entity we usually call "God." This is not disrespectful. Rather, to me, this acknowledges that the Almighty is likely far different from what our ancestors seemed to imagine two thousand years ago. Yet, this also suggests something else. When we consider what we now know about the *material* cosmos and imagine an eternal "spirit world," that likely has *not* changed but *we have*.

Early Greek philosophers theorized and debated the nature of the soul. One of the most incisive analyses of this is John Bussanich's 2013 "Rebirth and Eschatology in Plato and Plotinus" in the book *Philosophy and Salvation in Greek Religion*. There you would find concepts that sound familiar after you complete our book. An example is Plato's "River of Lethe" (i.e., Veil of Forgetfulness).

Also, in Bussanich's words, "The implicit constructive message of Platonic myth [i.e., writing] is that the rebirth cycle will continue without until one becomes detached from the desires and needs of the lower parts of the soul and seeks wisdom and virtue, even in the most constrained circumstances." Bussanich adds a statement of legitimacy for Plato's views, "I cannot defend the claim here, but the abundant evidence of mystical experiences in the [Platonic] dialogues demonstrates that Plato was intimately familiar with the transcendent worlds."

Your and My Souls

From experiential evidence, the soul joins the fetus in the womb. Soul consciousness manifests itself in the womb—remember Andrew Feldmar's four teenagers who repeatedly attempted suicide and the emotionally traumatic fetal memories addressed by the Association for Prenatal and Perinatal Psychology and Health?

Although *not* part of our normal awareness, our soul remains with us throughout our life and survives our physical death. As such, it experiences all that we experience. Being privy to our "unconscious" as well as to every conscious thought we ever have, our soul knows us better than we know ourselves.

It is important to mention here that—so long as our minds and bodies remain healthy—we are expected to continue our earthly lives. As suggested earlier, our souls are our links with the Almighty *and* are our God-given help for both the joys and sorrows of life on earth. It is through these times that our souls grow in spiritual wisdom, which is assessed by our Council of Elders in the afterlife.

Perhaps you are feeling somewhat overwhelmed that souls seem to have such an enormous *collective* responsibility to care for all of the Almighty's human creatures. But obvious to us all are the ways that many of us have strayed by pursuing only our pleasures, possessions, and power. Realizing that each of us seems to have an *immortal* soul therefore could come as an unwelcome shock to those who try to avoid punishment! While they may escape it during their lives on earth, their souls may suffer on an immortal scale. Remember the book's subtitle: "Whether You Like It or Not."

Remember that your soul is immortal and has capabilities you can't even imagine. Yet it *forces* you to do *nothing*. It simply and humbly invites you to realize that your soul's spiritual growth *can* lead to *its* greater responsibility in an everlasting reality *after* your human form is gone. Recall Michael Newton's comment earlier, "Thought patterns of the soul influence the human brain to induce motivations for certain actions."

So these new revelations about soul survival of mortal death may prompt anyone to learn more about his or her soul. This seems most productive if just sincerely intended rather than by seeking an immediate transformation. In other words, no one should expect an overnight change. At eighty-three years of age and having become soul-convinced less than a decade ago, I think I still am refining my conclusions gradually and carefully. Helping me do so are the remarkable and revolutionary reports continuing to emerge from experiential science, such as those you read in this book.

I still am not certain whether my daily behavior is always conscientiously shaped to comply with spiritual principles. I am better aware of them. But I feel that if I *mechanically* conform to them, this could become artificial. I therefore prefer to believe that my soul and I are developing a closer mutual understanding to help me recognize and increasingly try to learn about, and avoid, human frailties whenever possible. Remember, human frailties primarily involve how we treat others. Yet, we each should also protect our human bodies, to help them retain and offer our natural abilities to care for one another.

About now you likely wonder what other, more detailed, experiential evidence exists about souls. You nevertheless may question whatever is said— adults have had no awareness about their souls since very early childhood, even if then. So *disbelief* in souls is as natural as *belief* in things you can see, hear, touch, taste, and smell. Even considering that souls *may* exist might make you uncomfortable. Yet the hope of this book is that the indiscernible and inexplicable actuality of souls and the "spirit world" will be meaningful and reassuring. Remember that near-death survivors who "visited Heaven" begged to stay there, because they found it so appealing!

Council of Elders

Each soul "returning home" to the spirit world meets one or more times with its "Council of Elders." This first meeting is a review of the soul's self-account-ability for its most recent incarnation. So that appearance before the Council obviously is the one that souls fear. But each one knows that this is critical to its growth and development. Later meetings with the Council may help the soul plan its future incarnations in line with its karmic balance sheet and challenges remaining to be mastered.

This group of advanced souls exemplifies empathy and compassion—two traits that souls are expected to master through repeated incarnations on earth. Each soul has its own council to whom everything about it is totally transparent, so the soul is its own worst critic.

Part of the first meeting typically is a panoramic "full-screen" life review of the incarnation just completed. This has been described as involving everything that happened, including other people who were affected *from their point of view;* life-like sensations; and outcomes of alternative choices that might have been made. Yet, all of this is said to occur in what seems like an extremely short time by earth standards. Still, the Council is portrayed as forgiving, loving, compassionate, and supportive. But soul remorse is remarkably sincere, especially if its host body committed atrocious acts, like murder.

Individual souls therefore are encouraged to refrain from discussing their council meetings later with other souls—to "block" the participant-soul's thoughts—to maintain privacy. This seems to discourage "second-guessing" by fellow souls.

But council meetings in *no* way imply that "all is forgiven." Rather, souls whose human hosts egregiously and unconscionably mistreated others seem to be offered unusual options. One is to immediately reincarnate in "reverse" circumstances—to experience what its host's *victims* experienced in that life.

Another choice is solitary self-isolation for an extended period of time, even for many earth-lifetimes—thus penalizing that soul's progress. Obviously, this is a kind of "hell." A commentary appeared in a book that seems to illustrate this situation. But you should know that the book was psychically "communicated" over long breaks in time from a deceased Anglican nun to her living best friend, Helen Greaves. Yet, much of that book did contain information that seemed known only to the nun and Ms. Greaves. One passage involving the nun's continued spiritual work in Heaven, dealt with the dismal state of a soul in the pits of remorse. The nun expressed deep concern, believing that the soul's host might have been a Nazi perpetrator in the Holocaust.

However, when returning souls with minor infractions from their latest incarnation meet with their councils, council members may consider overwhelming causes for a soul's inability to influence its host's behavior—especially if efforts by the soul are apparent. This may involve the soul's maturity, its progress, and the challenges it faced. Also included, therefore, might be the host's mental state, his or her strengths and weaknesses, and any instinctive excesses. Any or all of these could influence the host's attitude toward and treatment of others *and* the soul's success or lack of it in influencing its host. However, failure could still require the soul to face the same challenges in a future incarnation.

Yet, because karma may seem rather strict for souls' self-accountability upon their "return home," council members consider many aspects of the soul, its host, and the nature of their life together. Apparently the soul is well aware that its primary goal is conquering fear of the human condition. This seems necessary in order to grow spiritually by overcoming negative emotions through perseverance over many lifetimes. But this often results in souls returning home bruised and hurt. Still, a soul's failure to master a human frailty may well require it to undergo one or more additional incarnations during which to overcome that shortcoming.

Also, a word of caution: no one escapes the problems of life on Earth by choosing to end it abruptly. The Council of Elders frowns upon suicide during a healthy life. It too can result in that soul having to relive the same challenges in its next incarnation.

Yet, on a positive note, council members also compliment souls for their hosts' specific acts of empathy, compassion, or benevolence toward others during their incarnation. Souls may have forgotten such individual instances but these were very evident to the council.

Soul Self-Accountability

God gives each of us a unique soul. Our soul therefore feels responsible to fulfill the three-fold intent of each incarnation: to learn; to develop spiritually; and to help its host. Only by being a part of the circumstances that confront humans, can souls learn why and how we act and react as we do. Naturally, our souls *usually* can view this with a much broader perspective than we humans can. This thereby may help both the soul and its host to avoid human frailties, like jealousy, hate, and vengeance.

The term "self-accountability" is so foreign to most of us that it deserves an explanation. Instead, some of us seem to pride ourselves in how much dishonesty we can "get away with," apparently justifying it to ourselves—and to others if we are caught—as "being deserved." Yet it may be no surprise that souls *willingly* manifest self-accountability, when we consider their many other remarkable characteristics and capabilities.

Soul self-accountability offers a different way to view the earthly concept of so-called "judgment," especially as the latter is often perceived as God's role to judge and punish human behavior. So you naturally wonder if there is *no* punishment for humans!

Think back to how God's punishment was portrayed in art, literature, and drama—bodies tortured relentlessly in hell. But you now should be able to realize that our physical bodies do *not* survive mortal death. Our souls do! This may confound your common sense. But God, Heaven, and your soul and mine seem to be part of the "other" reality that actually could exist *beyond the confines* of scientific materialism (i.e., physical world)!

Dead bodies are cremated or disintegrate in the grave! Moreover, since human bodies do *not* survive, anyone who expects special human privileges in Heaven as a sacrificial *martyr* will be sadly disappointed. Naturally, this will *not* be realized until perhaps too late to change!

Punishment of human bodies for heinous acts is reserved for criminal courts, and lesser gross behavior seems to be left to social mores. This approach acknowledges that human accountability may err in ways that leave some people only partially responsible or even irresponsible for their misconduct.

Soul self-accountability seems to have some humanly appealing characteristics:

- God's eminence is preserved as the eternal source of unconditional love.
- Self-accountability is consistent with human conduct that deserves judgment.
- Self-accountability perpetuates the purposes of human life—love and others.
- Souls' opportunities persist to try to positively influence their hosts' treatment of others.
- Our concern as souls emphasizes eternity, not just a single incarnation.

- Self-accountability remains the eternal gold standard for the behavior of all.

But souls apparently do have individual differences that distinguish them from one another, like humans do. This gives them weaknesses and strengths, again like humans. Depending upon the nature of the *mix* of soul and human characteristics in any incarnation, certain combinations seem more able to work together in successfully avoiding human pitfalls. Yet other mixes may involve negative, sometimes instinctive, human behavior that *attracts* the soul's weakness.

For example, a risk-taking, aggressive, or adventurous soul may become engrossed with its human host's life styles and emotions. Such a soul might become passively involved with a host body whose self-esteem feeds on power struggles for material gain without concern for others. That incarnation could fail to fulfill any of its three purposes. Later you will read how successes and failures from different incarnations are said to affect the soul's progress in a concept called "karma."

Yet, God never intended to punish—or to have any human religion punish—humankind for its frailties.

Spirit World

From the time of its origin, each soul somehow realizes it is a minute spark from the Creator. Thereafter, its all-consuming effort is to become worthy of rejoining the Source of All. But it understands that this *only* becomes possible once it has achieved full spiritual growth.

"Rejoining the Source of All" is naturally an elusive idea. Yet, the Almighty's wisdom might involve using the wisdom of advanced souls in the "administration" of Heaven. Consider, for example, that members of the many Councils of Elders would seem to fit this requirement.

Newton also stressed several principles that apply in the spirit world. First, space there is infinite, something we can't even imagine. Second, despite the population of billions of souls, there is a "structure and order to the spirit world also beyond human imagination." Third, the spirit world has unlimited access to energy forces designed to perform various operations more effectively and efficiently than anything that engineers can design on earth.

Newton writes that the ambience there "is a sublime matrix of compassion, harmony, ethics, and morality *far* beyond what we practice on earth." Ubiquitous harmony of spirit, honesty, humor, and love are the primary foundations of the spirit world. Because this is so different from what we know on earth, it may be hard to even imagine.

Various reports from "life-between-lives" spiritual regression subjects, and from near-death survivors, spoke of the spirit world as containing cities of light, spheres, beautiful gardens, fruit, magnificent buildings, homes, clothed entities resembling human form, lectures, study halls, and busy involvement in research, record keeping, and so forth.

Newton also says "everyone has a designated place in the spirit world." Perhaps it is obvious that the spirit world can address the needs of souls individually and in mass. That seems to reflect the overarching unconditional love of our Creator.

Newton's description about the spiritual care of each returning soul begins at the Gateway. Although souls of Newton's patients and clients may not have been involved in certain aspects of spirit world "operations," he stresses that invisible forces always are at work attending to *each* soul's specific needs. Souls in the spirit world work with peers who are at the same level of spiritual development in a planned and orderly self-development process.

Yet, there is one concept that seems all-embracing throughout the spirit world. It may help account for the soul's impetus for spiritual growth as well as to shield the privacy of the Divine. This concept is an idea of an eventual "union" of souls, hard to conceive using earth words. Nestled within this idea is the gradual spiritual advancement of souls toward making increasing contributions in the spirit world. Such a "union" might involve spiritually advanced individual souls and possibly some sort of coalescing of collective wisdom at even higher levels than council members.

The Presence

You probably have noticed that nothing so far in this book has described the Divinity—the One we call God or Allah. Metaphysical events may be "allowed" to show that we should not fear human death. Yet, even advanced souls (i.e., those no longer incarnating on earth) apparently don't have access to God or even to knowledge about the Almighty.

Nevertheless, Michael Newton's second book *Destiny of Souls* does contain almost two-dozen references to what is termed "The Presence." This is powerfully felt in souls' meetings with their Council of Elders. The Presence has been described as a "pulsating purple or violet light," perceptible to all spirit entities that attend such meetings. It apparently emanates from above (i.e., overhead of) the proceedings. When describing council meetings, subjects in a life-between-lives trance comment that their souls cannot focus on this light because it would distract them from discussions with council members.

The Presence is considered a "higher force," not necessarily singular or plural nor male or female. It apparently is representative of collective energy of infinite and eternal wisdom. Hypnotically regressed clients say that council members are the highest "power" (i.e., wisest ones) they encounter in the spirit world. But even council members don't seem to consider the Presence as the ultimate Divinity. No life-between-lives regressed subject has ever claimed to perceive or sense anything like "absolute perfection."

Nature of Souls

Souls have been described as bundles of "intelligent light energy." This may seem hard to imagine, but remember Cicoria's account earlier in the book. Being a scientist too, he was able to maintain his wits and remember details of his out-of-body experience. Bystanders saw his unconscious *human* body that had been thrown to the ground some distance from the phone. But they could *not* see his "energy body" that had separated and remained where the lightning hit him.

Experiential evidence describes souls as unique, individual, indestructible, non-material entities composed purely of spiritual energy—unlike any energy on earth—with a wide variety of amazing capabilities. Being in a state of spiritual energy, they are imperceptible to the five human senses, just like God and Heaven also are. Our souls therefore do not become part of the material composition of our bodies. Moreover, souls elude scientists' ability to characterize them in terms of classical physics.

Souls innately possess an apparently unlimited and unexcelled consciousness with conscience, imagination, honesty, intelligence, and special senses beyond human comprehension. Their creative capabilities are beyond our understanding too, allowing them to assume the physical appearance of humans. We should realize that, despite souls' immaterial composition, their ability to manipulate energy forces seems unlimited as "spirits." Yet souls seem able to acquire an even more sophisticated creative ability through specialized experience in the spirit world.

While in Heaven, they also can perceive, communicate, reason, learn, and move freely. Communication there occurs through something like telepathy (i.e., mental thought transfer). There too, souls are neither male nor female in terms of human understanding, but may incarnate in a male or female body.

No two souls are alike. Each has a unique immortal identity, according to various spiritual energy characteristics. This becomes its eternal identity and enables each soul to recognize one another. Perhaps this identity of our soul is what makes *you you* in your waking consciousness.

There is no hierarchy of souls in the spirit world. All are considered of equal value, but they differ in their level of development in spiritual wisdom and responsibility. Another variable is their degree of motivation. Still another is whether their energy becomes "contaminated" by their hosts' egregious acts. However, repair is possible.

Moreover, "thought energy"—a capability foreign to humans—seems to be the basis for many soul activities. Communication, creative skills, and even travel seem orchestrated by "thought." Newton says that an outstanding characteristic of the spirit world is "a continuous feeling of a powerful mental force facilitating everything in uncanny harmony." His patients and clients call the spirit world "a place of pure thought."

More specifically, each soul has a unique temperament and a set of traits all its own. Its identity is as distinguishing as a "fingerprint." This apparently relates to its formation, composition, and vibrational nature. This helps establish souls' individuality and enables them to recognize one another—despite the vast number of them.

For example, just as human beings are characterized using terms like "courageous," "quiet," "adventurous," "tenacious," "passive," "aggressive," "serious," "fun loving," "domineering," "action oriented," and "cautious," souls too are said to differ in their "soul-self." Moreover, they innately possess imagination, intuition, insight, and creativity far beyond anything on Earth—as well as that special attribute that we humans seem to have lost: conscience!

Yet, the character of each soul is immortal and may change only over multiple incarnations, whereas human traits can change over a single earth lifetime. It is important to match the soul's personality with the fetus' temperament, to improve the influence each may have on the other. Yet frailties exemplified by humans are not innate in the soul.

Soul Creativity

Michal Newton says that souls can create anything, as seems exemplified by this experience in the late Elizabeth Kubler-Ross' book *on LIFE after DEATH*. It is mind-blowing but her sincerity and integrity are unquestionable. It is from her 1977 speech "There Is No Death" in San Diego, California. She describes an unearthly experience that may illustrate the soul's unlimited creativity. Kubler-Ross had decided to quit her demanding work with death and dying patients. A woman approached her in the hall and asked to talk with her. But the psychiatrist had a strange feeling about the visitor. This person resembled a Mrs. Schwartz whom Kubler-Ross had known in her work, but that lady had died ten months earlier.

So, as they entered the office, the doctor touched the woman's skin, which seemed tangible enough. The visitor pleaded with Kubler-Ross not to forsake her work. Wisely, Kubler-Ross said, "You know Reverend Gaines is in Urbana now. He would just love to have a note from you. Would you mind?" She handed the woman a piece of paper and a pencil. After writing the note, the visitor frowned as if "Are you satisfied now?" as she handed it back to Kubler-Ross. When the woman stood up to leave, she repeated, "You promise?" Kubler-Ross' book reads, "And the moment I said, 'I promise,' she disappeared. We still have the note."

Not long ago I recalled an event in my life that happened while I was still a young skeptic. Back then I simply discounted that experience with nothing more than great relief and gratitude. In light of Kubler-Ross' experience, I now wonder. At that time, my mother had been hospitalized twice and eventually was unable to care for herself. So I hurried to her apartment back in Virginia to see what could be done. Hopelessly mired in doubt and worry, I heard a knock on the apartment door. There stood a huge middle-aged woman in simple, plain clothes, with a small, scruffy suitcase in one hand. She said simply, "I'm here to care for your mother." Awestruck, I welcomed her in.

For the next year or so this woman took over all responsibilities for Mama. She slept on a futon, cashed Mama's Social Security checks, paid the rent and utility bills, and shopped, cleaned, and cooked for my mother. She had a rather gruff way about her, kept to herself, and wouldn't engage in conversation. She refused to be paid.

When Mama was taken to the hospital again and I was told she would need nursing home care, I rushed home to close the apartment, move her furniture out, and make other necessary arrangements. The woman had disappeared without saying anything to anyone. To this day no one knows who she was, where she came from, or where she went. Nor did anyone ever speak of seeing her. I now consider her some sort of compassionate spiritual being.

Soul Groups and Activities

Souls begin in a "primary" group of about seven members. This enables each of them to know one another well and to develop close bonds that last forever. Members of each primary group are basically at the same level of development. But each soul also has individual strengths and weaknesses as well as a different potential for growth and degree of motivation. It seems that primary cluster groups are somehow composed of assorted types for balance. Any souls who develop faster may be moved to more advanced groups, but will never forget their primary group "buddies." Remember Newton's patient who got so lonely, missing fellow members in her primary group?

Souls that may have incarnated "together"—for example in different hosts, living at a similar earth time, or "connected" as family or extended family members—also develop close relationships in the spirit world. Such affiliations form so-called "secondary groups" of a thousand or more souls.

During its eternal existence at home in the spirit world, each soul interacts with countless other souls. This enables many groups to become very close-knit and may involve so-called soul mates. Souls will also meet with spirit guides, teachers, and counselors. They can participate in a wide variety of activities, for further learning, recreation, and service. They also may have time alone for thought and development. Special "immersion" experiences are available to sharpen sensitivity to other forms of life or to recharge soul energy.

But regardless of a soul's stage of development, each one treats all other souls with humility, respect, conviviality, and dignity. Souls are said to value honesty with themselves and with other souls as a prime virtue. They seek and welcome feedback from other souls as a means of spiritual growth. They willingly offer feedback to other souls, completely devoid of judgment. That growth is central to each soul's existence.

In the spirit world, advanced souls may have an unusual ability and opportunity to demonstrate compassion, love, caring, and empathy. Therefore, they may be recognized and respected for those talents in counseling and helping less advanced souls. The unconditional love demonstrated by souls for one another is unparalleled on earth. It is best considered a reflection of the total love and acceptance exemplified by our Creator.

The opportunities for growth, specialization, and service in Heaven are viewed by souls with great humility. Examples are said to include Nursery Teachers, Harmonizers, Masters of Design, Explorers, and Archivists. Very advanced souls therefore may not need to reincarnate.

Spirit Guides

Angels have been a part of religious lore forever. Many persons tell of life-threatening circumstances from which they were rescued by unseen forces or excruciating times through which they were consoled. Spirit guides are assigned to each incarnating soul. The one possible common denominator for all such sources of help might best be called "spirit entities." Reports from Newton's clients account for spirit entities in a variety of roles. These more advanced entities seem able to help souls in special ways:

- watching over incarnated souls,
- escorting returning souls through the "tunnel" or meeting and comforting them at what Newton calls the "Gateway,"
- reorienting returning souls to the spirit world,
- joining them in their appearance before the council, counseling souls in need of help, and
- assisting them in planning for reincarnation.

"Advanced" typically means souls who likely have achieved optimal spiritual growth, no longer need to incarnate, and have participated in special training. One of Newton's clients said "we are always protected, supported, and directed within the system by master souls."

Transition and Placement

Newton's first book spent two chapters on these aspects of souls returning home. This involves gathering and movement of returning souls to specific groups in the spirit world. Large numbers of returning souls apparently are conveyed in a spiritual form of mass transit to their proper destinations. Newton comments that an outstanding characteristic of the spirit world is "a continuous feeling of a powerful mental force facilitating everything in uncanny harmony." Perhaps it is obvious by now that the spirit world can address the needs of souls individually and in mass.

Destinations

At the intended destinations, souls are said to debark the spiritual mass transit into the space reserved for their colony, composed of a specific group of souls at their own maturity level. Souls in these cluster groups are intimate old friends from previous incarnations who have about same awareness level, who have direct and frequent contact. But not all of the souls whose hosts are close to us in our earthly lives are on same developmental level in Heaven.

All Work and No Play?

Michael Newton's book *Destiny of Souls* contains a section entitled "Leisure Time," acknowledging that the afterlife (i.e., Heaven) also offers leisure time, including recess breaks from learning, occasional quiet solitude, recreational or educational trips, and visits with beloved deceased pets, as well as dancing, music, and games that foster camaraderie among residents.

About now, you may have a greater appreciation for your awesome soul and its soul consciousness. Perhaps you also realize that your soul, like your human consciousness, is unique—no other soul is like yours. Said differently, in your spiritual state none other is like you! There too, you have your individual identity and personality. There, however, you are immortal. There, you have a creative ability beyond earthly imagination. In addition to the many pleasant aspects that reminded NDE survivors of earth, the ambience in Heaven is said to be of incomparable beauty, peace, love, fellowship, joy, and honesty.

However, you may have anxiety about encountering the soul of someone with whom you had an unpleasant relationship on earth. Recognize that this may have resulted from that person's or your own ego, which are left behind at death. Regardless, it is a tenet of Heaven to help resolve any such lingering difficulties, with assistance from fellow souls.

At this moment, you likely feel overwhelmed by what you are reading. The idea of having a soul might seem foreign, perhaps even threatening. You and I grew up knowing that "reality" is what we *can* see, touch, hear, taste, and smell. That naturally gives us a feeling of security. Yet the "unknown" has been with us forever. So the next chapter discusses the two interdependent concepts of reincarnation and karma.

Thirteen

REINCARNATION AND KARMA

"It is in giving that we receive,
it is in loving that we are loved,
it is in forgiving that we are forgiven,
and ultimately it is in dying that we live."

ST. FRANCIS OF ASSISI

S t. Francis' words seem understandable. Yet, their implications escape those who are concerned *only* with this lifetime. The underlying essence here is "karma." It has a specific meaning for reincarnation and soul immortality.

One of the implications of soul consciousness is reincarnation—the "repeated incarnation" of individual souls into different host bodies for different lifetimes on earth. Another is for humans to acknowledge the preeminence of the soul to the human body in terms of survival of mortal death and self-accountability. A third is for humans to recognize that the soul's passion for spiritual growth and wisdom is intimately associated with the human host's culpability on earth.

Note: this is one of the chapters that address one of the two *other* objectives of this book cited in the Introduction: "the brash *willingness* by terrorists to seek death for *false* promises of reward in Heaven."

Reincarnation is probably the concept with which most Western cultures have trouble. This may have been the reason for German philosopher Friedrich Nietzsche's terse claim later at the beginning of the next chapter on immortality:

"Live so that thou mayest desire to live again – that is thy duty – for in any case thou wilt live again!"

Therefore, inquiring about your soul, especially early in life, could offer you additional meaning, just as actual-death experiences (ADEs) offer their survivors new hope. But you may have read that ADE survivors' spiritual conversion may pose problems with their families and friends on earth. Apparently these other people felt much less comfortable with survivors' new beliefs, attitude, and behavior. Is it possible that at least a few of these "others" conscientiously became uncomfortable with their *own* life styles?

As a skeptic of the paranormal for most of my life, I would have disavowed everything you are reading in this book, certainly the existence of a "soul" or "soul consciousness" within me! However, I now feel that these are real, not just from my research, but from my personal experiences during the last few years. I have received many intuitive "nudges"—that I now consider soul messages—all of which have been beneficially productive. Also, as I look back over my eighty-three years, as I faced a great many fork-in-the-road options, none of my choices have disappointed me. Some outcomes have required time for reflection in later years, but each one left me feeling that synchronicity was at work all along.

Many of you may feel that souls are unfairly blamed for their hosts' thoughts and actions. Obviously our lack of awareness of our souls leaves us free to pursue personal self-gratification at the expense of others. True, some of us have temperaments that blend with our souls to produce personalities that allow us to manifest empathy, compassion, and benevolence. But there are just as many or more of us who, for whatever reasons, live without regard to the consequences of our thoughts and actions. Perhaps the latter truly believe that we will live only once.

A Christian minister once told me he thought that being reincarnated is the worst kind of punishment. I suspected that he had experienced a tough childhood. Now, however, I can see his viewpoint—he just didn't carry his explanation far enough. Reincarnation is a commitment for immortality—our souls experience earthly lessons that will help their spiritual growth. Remember that souls who achieve wisdom through multiple reincarnations are given greater responsibility in the spirit world.

The minister was correct that rebirth is not easy for the human infant or for the soul. Yet, training and participating in the Olympics is not easy either. Still, from the soul's point of view, the challenge and the achievement from reincarnation are just as great as becoming an Olympic Gold Medalist.

Also consider that reincarnation is not haphazard. Our souls have the opportunity to choose their new hosts' family and circumstances into which to be born. Remember too Chamberlain's reports of memories from the womb which stretch back before conception.

Before Reincarnation

Robert Schwartz's *Your Soul's Plan: Discovering the Real Meaning of the Life You Planned Before You Were Born* is just one of the books on this subject. This encompasses the idea that each soul typically selects a purpose for its life on earth. This may relate to its inability to have mastered certain human frailties.

Yet life plans also may be made *not* for spiritual growth of *that* soul but to assist in the spiritual growth of others: parents, other family members, or even friends. When we see persons who are victims of great adversity, this does not *necessarily* mean they were perpetrators of evil or wrongdoing in a former life. For example, a soul may volunteer to incarnate in a life it knows will be shortened by an incurable disease in order to help others learn empathy and compassion.

A prime example lived among us not long ago. People of many nations are aware of this young person, who almost certainly must have been a living model of such a soul. This was Mattie Stepanek, who died in 2004 at age thirteen from the terminal effects of dysautonomic mitochondrial myopathy, a rare disorder. Anyone who has read Mattie's poetry, owned his books, or seen his personal appearances must have felt a tug at their heartstrings for this child. Often on the *Oprah* show, his upbeat, genial manner seemed oblivious to the life-support tubes he wore everywhere.

He had a kindly philosophy of life, of people, of nature, and the world in general. He certainly reached far beyond the understanding not only of a child his age but also beyond that of many adults. In a personal communication from his mother, Jeni, she told me that, from the time he was a small child, Mattie felt that his "purpose for being on earth was to be a messenger, to make people smile despite challenges." Incidentally, Jeni's book revealed that her four children all had this disease and three died at younger ages than Mattie. Jeni has the adult-onset variety of the disease.

Remember the "veil of forgetfulness"? A fascinating quote from the distant past echoes how the soul's role in life selection may have unintended consequences for its host later in life. James Hillman's book *The Soul's Code: In Search of Character and Calling* quotes Plotinus (205-270 CE) that "we elected the body, the parents, the place, and the circumstances that suited the soul [which] suggests that the circumstances, including my body and my parents whom I may curse ... I do not understand because I have forgotten [therefore] we must attend very carefully to childhood to catch early glimpses of the [soul] in action, to grasp its intentions and not block its way."

Soul Reincarnation

The soul's eventual goal is to reach ultimate spiritual maturity primarily through its incarnated experiences. But there are reports that learning also occurs in the spirit world, with the help of soul teachers and other specialist souls. Still, all souls agree that earthly incarnation remains the best experience for learning. Whatever your attitude toward souls' repeated incarnations on earth, you should agree that God's intent is exquisitely straightforward and relatively simple. This seems to be part of "life's ultimate mystery."

Souls reincarnate in different bodies over many earth-lifetimes to learn to overcome human frailties in how we treat one another. Remember that all human frailties involve our thoughts, intentions, and actions toward others. In that plan, our souls seem to be God's agents in caring for His creations.

Another item of possible surprise is that souls apparently do not reincarnate in the same direct hereditary family they had in past lives, according to Michael Newton. But members of the same larger soul groups may choose new families where they can be together. They tend to be associated by indirect blood ties and geographic proximity.

But consider, of course, that each soul may spend many earth-lifetimes to achieve spiritual growth, whereas each of its hosts is allowed only a small fraction of that eternity. Only as our souls achieve the wisdom that comes with spiritual growth can they join other spiritually advanced souls in being given greater responsibilities in the spirit world (i.e., Heaven). This may help explain the necessity of our soul's repeated incarnations to "get it right"—to help its hosts realize that God's plan is for each of us to love and care for one another.

Consider if you had the responsibility of setting up such a massive-scale community of humans and assuring everyone of your timeless concern for their welfare, would you have done it any differently than through their souls? If you feel it should be through divine intervention instead, how far out on the limb of human risk should such intervention occur? How often? For everyone, or only a few?

The process of reincarnation is still hidden in mystery, with experiential evidence only becoming available as discussed in earlier chapters. But even this evidence can go only so far in helping humankind accept, acknowledge, and respect the majesty of the sacred.

Souls are said to be capable of exploring the fetus' neurophysiology to ascertain its and its mother's mental and physical health. Then, at some time, the soul and the human self do seem to begin to work together to shape the person's personality. After this, both the soul and the self are a part, almost as one, of the individual's life—his or her thoughts, intentions, and actions.

This kind of outcome of such a relationship is naturally the most optimistic scenario. You certainly would realize this as you see extremes of greed, selfishness, malevolence, jealousy, power and wealth hunger, self-gratification, and other human frailties existing around you. Some comments therefore are in order to qualify the "perfect relationship."

Each infant is subject to genetic inherited traits, possibly including any abnormal brain chemistry. Each also is influenced by insufficiency of nurturing and by any mental or physical abuse. When these occur before three years of age, subconscious emotional trauma may exist which, if unresolved, may turn into frank lifelong mental disorders, behavior problems, or even malevolence. Each soul, although innately without fault, has its own characteristic temperament. Negative emotions also may persist from earlier incarnations, sometimes burdening the soul with guilt. Obviously, these and other difficulties may interfere with an effective merger of soul and human self.

Soul Development

As a result, having the body "self" accept the soul "self" as a partner can be difficult, especially for a young or immature soul. Apparently, however, "young" souls are not left alone and may need help from "soul guides" in adjusting to their human hosts. But all immature souls are not "young." Rather, immaturity is a stage of the soul's spiritual growth over multiple incarnations on earth. "Young" souls may have had only one or two incarnations.

Past-life researchers and therapists apparently have hypnotically regressed some patients and clients to Stone Age lives, thousands of years ago. Of course, some souls may incarnate less frequently than others. However, the idea that souls may continue to reincarnate over time suggests that some have had greater difficulty than others in mastering human frailties. But recognize, too, that the development of humankind has grown increasingly ego-driven in ways that early humans could not have imagined. This then makes life on earth today much more challenging for souls.

Veil of Forgetfulness

Acknowledging soul self-accountability could seem to be more humanly demanding, since our souls are eternal, yet they are part of us that we likely deny because of the legendary "veil of forgetfulness." The Christian New Testament quotation most often referred to in Satterfield's online references to the veil is from the Apostle Paul's first letter to the Corinthians 13:12 "For now we see through a glass, darkly; but then face to face: now I know in part; but then shall I know even as also I am known." This appears to contrast human consciousness before, and soul consciousness after, death of the mortal body. It therefore seems quite possible that our souls hold the answer to two haunting questions: "Why am I here?" and "Is this all there is to life?"

Realizing the reality of our souls should help persuade each of us that we are much more than our body, our personality, our achievements, our possessions—and, likewise—than our wealth, power, and privilege. We all are eternally connected through our souls.

But the "veil" keeps us from being consciously aware of our soul and soul memories, so our souls cannot use lessons learned in past incarnations to avoid similar challenges in the current life.

Past Lives

Reincarnation is inextricably linked with the idea of past lives, and it was a common belief during Jesus' time. But the First Council of Nicaea, called by Constantine in 325 AD, established the consensus of Christian canons. The Council selected, from among the books then being circulated about Jesus and the apostles, the ones that are today recognized as the Christian New Testament.

In his book *Reincarnation in Christianity: A New Vision of the Role of Rebirth in Christian Thought*, Geddes MacGregor delves into the annals of Christian history to demonstrate that Christian doctrine and reincarnation are not mutually exclusive belief systems. MacGregor believes that the Church rejected reincarnation not for theological reasons but as a threat to the Church and to Rome at a time when their institutional strength was crucial. He is Emeritus Distinguished Professor of Philosophy at the University of Southern California.

Moreover, reincarnation has been a common belief for thousands of years among orthodox Jews. Therefore it was a common belief in Jesus' time. However, early Church Fathers who were accused of teaching reincarnation had their works banned.

Science and much of the public disavow reincarnation and past lives, just as they do out-of-body and actual-death experiences. Yet OBEs, ADEs, and past lives have been experientially demonstrated in countless ways. This chapter therefore offers seeming examples of reincarnation for which no alternate explanation appears acceptable.

Memories From the Past

A remarkable account of reincarnations of Jews who died in the Holocaust was provided in Rabbi Yonassan Gershom's first book, *Beyond the Ashes: Cases of Reincarnation from the Holocaust* (1992). His second book, *From Ashes to Healing: Mystical Encounters with the Holocaust* (1996), provided firsthand accounts from fourteen people who suffered traumatic memories of the Holocaust. He stressed the idea that souls usually reincarnate within the culture they inhabited in prior lifetimes, but some of these stories are from Gentiles who may have had Jewish ancestors. Rabbi Gershom reinforced the idea that reincarnation teachings were preserved and still are being taught by the ultraorthodox Hasidim.

University of Virginia professor of psychiatry Ian Stevenson devoted over forty years to carefully investigating and documenting more than two thousand cases of very young children who spontaneously remembered past lives. His 2000 book *Children Who Remember Previous Lives: A Question of Reincarnation* is a compelling report on his detailed analyses.

Some of Stevenson's young subjects spoke of being fathers or husbands and gave names of their children or wives. They also described where they had lived. Sure enough, when the professor interviewed those identified in their homes, their names and the characteristics of the homes matched what the children had said. If the child accompanied the researcher, the child often recognized past-life family members and called them by name.

Xenoglossy

One of the puzzling aspects of reincarnation is what is known as "xenoglossy." This is an apparent ability to speak fluently one or more foreign languages without having been exposed to them in this lifetime.

Stevenson devoted two books to xenoglossy. In one book, *Unlearned Language: New Studies in Xenoglossy,* he described the case of a thirty-seven-year-old woman who, under hypnosis, reverted to the speech and manner of a male. She spoke fluent Spanish, although she did not do so in a normal state of consciousness. Stevenson studied this woman for eight years and was unable to find an explanation through his usual meticulous investigative techniques.

In her book *Reincarnation: The Phoenix Fire Mystery*, Sylvia Cranston described the case of twin baby boys, children of the prominent New York physician Marshall W. McDuffie and his wife, Wilhelmina. The twins were heard talking to one another in a language that neither parent recognized. When the boys continued to do so, they were taken to the foreign language department of Columbia University, but no one there could identify it. A professor of ancient languages happened to hear them and identified it as Aramaic, a tongue spoken at the time of Jesus.

Other researchers in past life hypnotic regression have even reported that, when the subjects told of past lives in different cultures, they sometimes were able to speak in the language that was native to the particular culture at that time.

While discussing this with nurses at an Indianapolis hospital, I was told about an unusual case there. This involved an American with severe head injuries from a motorcycle accident. Before recovery, he was recorded speaking in fluent German. After recovery, he was unable to do so, never having learned the language.

Child Prodigies

Another equally puzzling aspect of reincarnation is child prodigy. Child prodigies have shown amazing abilities in mathematics, music, and other fields. In one of his many books, *How to Know God,* Deepak Chopra wrote, "People who spend time with geniuses and prodigies often find them unearthly ... as if a very old soul has been confined to a new body and yet brings in experience far beyond what that body could have known."

Scott Pelley interviewed such a young musical prodigy on CBS's 60 Minutes on November 28, 2006. At twelve, the young man, Jay Greenberg, had already written five full-length symphonies. Sam Zyman, who taught Jay music theory at Juilliard School in New York City, had taught there for eighteen years. He said that Jay "is a prodigy of the level of the greatest prodigies in history ... the likes of Mozart, Mendelssohn, and Saint-Sans." Jay said the compositions just appear in his head and he writes them down, even though he may not be able to play them. He wrote "The Storm," commissioned by the New Haven Symphony in Connecticut, in just a few hours.

Child prodigies have occurred throughout history and elicited awe and speculation. Doctors Lehndorff and Falkenstein told about a young boy from Lubeck, Denmark named Christian Henrich Heineken. In 1723, at two years of age, he had already become fluent in French and Latin. By three, he had written a history of Denmark, and by four, he had become a brilliant mathematician. He died of natural causes half a year later. This appeared in the 1955 *Archives of Pediatrics*.

Implications of Reincarnation

Theologian Christopher Bache, professor of religious studies at Youngstown State University, suggested that reincarnation has provided a vital missing link in Western theology: "Theologians have never satisfactorily explained the purpose of suffering in a universe created by a loving God, nor why it is so inequitably distributed." But remember Mattie Stepanek, whose soul may have sacrificially chosen his brief life to help others grow spiritually? In his book *Lifecycles: Reincarnation and the Web of Life*, Bache also wrote, "It's ironic, really. Christianity has taught us that God, the name given the Ultimate Reality in life, is loving, benevolent, and completely trustworthy. Yet it has also taken from us the key we need to recognize this love."

Some theologians seem to feel that reincarnation may cause those who believe in it to feel able to dispense with the institutional aspects of the Christian Way. But remember that this was a common belief during Jesus' time. My own belief now is that the entire concept of soul, spirit world, and reincarnation stresses the importance of love in our relationships with one another, and that our lives are inexorably intertwined. The church provides the gathering place where we can learn and practice these important principles and reach out to others who need our help. If religious institutions embraced the existence of souls too, they could offer invaluable guidance in spiritual practice wherein their members could help rather than hinder their souls' development.

If a soul reincarnates, remember that it has the opportunity in the spirit world to first preview and select from among different bodies, personalities, environments, and even parents. Humans naturally consider any such claim nonsensical! Yet it might be true if Heaven is timeless—apparently no "before" or "after" existing there.

So it may be no wonder that people may complain later about family mistreatment on Earth. They "forget" that their souls made the selection. What's more, those experiences may be part of his or her soul's spiritual growth. Newton's clients stress, "The real lessons of life are learned by recognizing and coming to terms with being human."

Supposedly, souls planning a new incarnation do so in keeping with the karmic principles of spiritual growth through the exercise of free will. That is, they may select a life that offers an opportunity to grow from an injustice or wrong committed in an earlier incarnation. Or they may choose a life that offers an opportunity to experience poverty and learn gratitude, experience greed and learn selflessness, or experience abuse and learn compassion, from among many choices.

Karma

Reincarnation is accompanied by a concept called "karma." It holds an established position in Hinduism and Buddhism as "the ethical consequences of one's actions." Karma has differing meanings, especially between Eastern traditions and Western interpretations. In the Buddhist and Hindu sense, karmic actions will bear fruit at some future time, implicitly for the person or his or her family or descendents. But in the spiritual sense, our words, thoughts, and actions are charged against or credited to our soul. The term "karma" has been applied to the overall concept, to specific circumstances, and to individual behavior. Basically, it apparently involves debits or credits, like a bank account, that the soul accumulates over various incarnations.

Karma in the spiritual interpretation may seem harsh since our souls are held responsible for their hosts' treatment of others in each incarnation. Our lack of awareness or disavowal of our souls apparently makes no difference to karma. Souls seem to incarnate for the lessons they can learn about human nature—why and how human frailties occur. Each and every frailty involves how we treat others: jealousy, vengeance, retribution, envy, lust, and fraud—just to name a few.

Soul incarnation on earth is also intended to help each of us better understand and overcome human frailties. Furthermore, our souls' spiritual growth also comes from avoiding being caught up in their hosts' mistreatment of other people. Therefore, perhaps the underlying spiritual intent of karma is to reflect our souls' *efforts* —or lack of them—to positively influence their hosts' concern for others *without* becoming ensnared in their hosts' personal frailties.

For example, a soul "credit" might have been achieved for the Good Samaritan's actions in the Christian New Testament in caring for a fellow traveler's distress. Apparently, a "debit" could be charged to the souls whose hosts ignored the same traveler's distress. Interestingly, when a malevolent act between two persons is forgiven by the one harmed, it is said that this may relieve the offender's soul of karmic debt.

Essentially, karma acknowledges that souls' passion is growth in spiritual wisdom. This seems evident because of their affinity with God; their recognition of humankind's universal connectedness through our souls; and their realization of the attributes of spiritual practices in all human relationships. Souls' spiritual development and growth are the pathways to greater responsibility in the spirit world. The soul's achievement might be prized as personally as an Olympian win but without a gold medal or endorsement contracts. If this seems to be the ultimate expression of humility, it is.

In his book *Destiny of Souls*, Michael Newton offers this observation: "Although karma is associated with justice, its essence is not punitive but one of bringing balance to the sum of our deeds in all past lives."

We naturally are unable to know the spirit world's actual assessment of souls' efforts and progress. However, it seems reasonable that council members would consider certain facts about each soul and its host. Any and all of these could influence the host's attitude toward and treatment of others *and* the soul's success or lack of it in influencing its host:

- Soul's maturity.
- Soul's level of spiritual growth.
- Soul's mesh with host's temperament.
- Soul's weaknesses and strengths.
- Host's implicit or repressed memories that threaten interpersonal relationships.
- Host's organic or genetic brain defects.
- Host's extent of its own nurturance and self-esteem.
- Host's social and emotional maturity.
- Intensity of host's instinct and ego drives.

Edgar Cayce, the "sleeping prophet," claimed that thoughts, rather than actions or failures, trigger karma. This may be doubted, but it does appear that thought energy is a currency of the cosmos, as supposedly is recorded in the Akashic field (i.e., spiritual Books of Life). For example, consider that the shared-death experience for a family to participate in their loved one's passing may be accompanied by a panoramic "life review" of memories from the life just lived. What better way to accept this than as a thought-energy based sort of "video replay"? Such "energy" seems far different from the ones known by science. But it may relate to the nature of souls and to medical cases known as "healing touch."

Many "near-death" survivors and subjects of spiritual (i.e., life-between-lives) regression insist that we all are "one" (i.e., united). This book enables you to understand their claim—for souls! Yet the worldwide diversity of humankind argues against this for human beings. So consider that "karma" reaches inside each of us to our God-given soul, beyond all of our physical and mental *human* nature.

Yet, consider too, that through our souls, all six to seven billion of us *are* "connected." We all are part of a common *spiritual* heritage. Obviously, this does *not* mean that a teacher in Los Angeles is "connected" to a fisherman in Taiwan. Nevertheless, during the course of each human lifetime for any specific geographical area, each person will cross the path of another person any number of times. But for any two people, each may encounter the other only once. For two who have a close relationship, the number of times may seem unlimited. Regardless, each of us carries to, and each takes away from, every interaction something of benefit or harm to the other person. It may be as seemingly insignificant as a smile or a frown, a greeting or a curse, or a kiss or slap in the face.

Regardless, the behavior of *others toward us*—anger versus warmth, manipulation versus support, hatred versus tolerance, and so on—typically causes us to react. The *way* we react can reinforce negative karma or neutralize it. Responding to anger with anger, for example, even if only with our thoughts and feelings, perpetuates negative karma.

However, have you ever noticed how the other person's antagonistic mood and behavior can change dramatically if you react *differently* from how he or she expects? There is no such thing as one person arguing, just as there is no one hand clapping. Of course, this means that we must avoid getting "caught up in the moment," so to speak. This applies *whenever* we make *any* decision about, or launch any action toward, another person—each of us naturally has dormant animal instincts that all too often govern our relationships with other people.

Free Will Versus Determinism

Karma obviously seems to result from free will. This book suggests that both souls and human beings have free will and that, through this, the Almighty granted human beings the ability to attain their human potential. But free will has been debated down through the ages. Therefore this discussion seems worthwhile.

Souls apparently can choose the host and circumstances into which to be born. They also seem able to adjust the frequency of their incarnations according to their need and degree of motivation for spiritual development.

Although some scriptural accounts claim direct involvement of the Divine Source in human welfare, this book suggests that, after mankind was put on earth, each individual was *primarily* responsible for his or her own behavior. This recognizes:

- That external influences naturally *can affect* human choices.
- That humans may be *required* to comply with decisions of other people.
- But that an individual's *response* to non-binding circumstances in which a person finds him- or herself offers possible choices, granting human potential.

Remember, each and every thought, action, and consequence, no matter how seemingly trivial, is said to be registered in the Hall of Records and is known to the Omniscient Presence we call God. Parenthetically, this archive seems compatible with the idea of invisible fields, such as the Akashic Field described by Ervin Laszlo.

Service is fundamental to karma. So the Council also emphasizes commendable actions that provide karmic credit. One report involved the Council asking a soul about the "bus-stop incident." The soul apparently didn't remember, so the Council described it: "You stepped off a bus, late and in a hurry. You noticed a woman sitting on a bench in the rain, crying and looking forlorn. So you sat beside her, raised your umbrella, and put your arm around her, trying to comfort her."

"Natural" Compassion and Benevolence

Moreover, it is noteworthy that natural disasters create an outpouring of compassion and benevolence. Devastation by tornadoes, hurricanes, and tsunamis, for example, quickly bring help from otherwise "ordinary persons," often unknown to victims. Volunteers offer assistance, food, clothing, and even temporary shelter. What seems remarkable is that this occurs *without* volunteers ever questioning the cost or time they might spend. Moreover, examples often appear in local news media of *spontaneous* heroism in rescuing the driver from a burning or sinking automobile. All of these certainly must be *experiential* evidence of "unconscious" soul influences—likely even without the *benefactor* realizing that he or she was "soul-motivated"! Or do these examples reveal that compassion and benevolence exist in each of us, hidden by a veneer of artificiality?

Some researchers spoke of karma as the result of human host interactions over all incarnations of the soul. It was said that a soul could acquire several kinds of debits or credits in each lifetime as a result of the impact of its human host on other persons' lives. Supposedly, these so-called debits and credits can be balanced through succeeding lifetimes on earth as a tool for spiritual growth of the soul.

Karma and Malevolence

When one considers the world at large, karma and immortality seem to be *disregarded* in widespread malevolence. But karma does acknowledge that the soul's passion for spiritual growth and wisdom is intimately associated with its human hosts' culpability.

Malevolence obviously is the extreme of a range of thoughts, words, and actions of ill will. This spectrum is inherent in disregard for others, a common human frailty. Still, some offenders might try to rationalize their behavior as having only one lifetime or as their concern for survival.

But any book claiming to address science and religion must certainly consider other changes occurring in our world today. So, although malevolence might emerge from individual feelings of insecurity or lack of both self-worth and love during early childhood, it also may be shaped by group efforts for world domination.

It may seem harsh, but is crucial to accept, that human religious leaders occasionally misuse their influence on their followers' beliefs and practices.

Remember Jim Jones, leader of the Peoples Temple, and their mass suicide in Guyana in 1978? Recall, too, the armed Crusades begun by Pope Urban II in 1095 CE?

Whitton's "life-between-lives" participants therefore said that karma essentially is learning, as ordained by our Creator. Obviously, this learning results from a variety of life experiences, some of them naturally painful. We tread the uncertain paths of life on earth, seemingly out of touch with our souls in exerting our free will choices. No wonder that the *absence* of "divine" interventions causes some people to disbelieve in God; to feel that God has abandoned them; or to insist that God is dead. At the time of a calamity our human focus is on "Why?" However, the soul takes the long view and measures its spiritual growth over many human lifetimes.

Akashic Records

One of Ervin Laszlo's books focuses on an "interconnecting cosmic field at the roots of reality that conserves and conveys information, known as the Akashic record," according to its Amazon description. Michael Newton writes, "Souls typically find their permanent records of past-life accomplishments and shortcomings stored in places resembling earthly libraries. Indian philosophy uses this term [i.e., Akashic] to describe a space representing a universal filing system that records every thought, word, and action in our lifetime." This, then, might be where our karmic balance sheets are stored.

As this book acknowledges, we not only are *unaware* of our souls but we also typically pursue instinct and ego drives that serve our perceived "best interests." Only by honestly considering that we *might* have a soul and that this *might* have some worthwhile meaning for our loved ones and us, is anyone *likely* to give this book much further thought? In that case, one final question remains: "Do our souls communicate with us?

The next chapter examines the immortality of your soul and mine, as suggested in this book's title. But the chapter after that one it is entitled "Messages From Our Souls."

Fourteen

IMMORTALITY

"Live so that thou mayest desire to live again –
that is thy duty –
for in any case thou wilt live again!"

FRIEDRICH NIETZSCHE

*N*one of us can even imagine what immortality is like, because it obviously occurs one life at a time. Yet, some futurists perennially promise ways to achieve *human* immortality—more politely called "life extension"—perpetuating hope of avoiding mortal death.

Reasons to seek *human* immortality abound. Some individuals with substantial fortunes already attempt to be remembered in perpetuity by funding family-named institutions. Patriarchs in large, wealthy families may worry that their children and grandchildren will waste their hard-earned riches. Many people are concerned how their offspring will fare without them.

Note: this is a chapter that addresses one of the two *other* objectives of this book cited in the Introduction: "the brash *willingness* by terrorists to seek death for *false* promises of reward in Heaven."

The Immortal Soul

The *Catholic Encyclopedia* offers a frank assessment of human belief in the soul:

> "Various theories as to the nature of the soul have claimed to be reconcilable with the tenet of immortality, but it is a sure instinct that leads us to suspect every attack on the substantiality or spirituality of the soul as an assault on the belief in existence after death. The soul may be defined as the ultimate internal principle by which we think, feel, and will, and by which our bodies are animated. That our vital activities proceed from a principle capable of subsisting in itself is the thesis of the substantiality of the soul: that this principle is not itself composite, extended, corporeal, or essentially and intrinsically dependent on the body, is the doctrine of spirituality. If there be a life after death, clearly the agent or subject of our vital activities must be capable of an existence separate from the body. The belief in an animating principle in some sense distinct from the body is an almost inevitable inference from the observed facts of life."

"Whether You Like It Or Not!"

But remember this subtitle of the book? Obviously, this implies that none of us have a choice about our souls. Therefore, *if* you believe that you *might* possibly have a God-given soul, this book should have helped you better understand its implications *and* its promises for your loved ones and for you. But, if you prefer to wait to find out after your body dies *or* if you insist on denying that you have a soul, please realize that everyone seems to have a soul—"whether you like it or not!"

Immortality Project

Perhaps the most forward-reaching effort of combined disciplines interested in immortality is a current project at the University of California at Riverside.

It is entitled "The Science, Philosophy, and Theology of Immortality." It was supported by a grant from the John Templeton Foundation in 2014. The project leader is John Martin Fischer, Riverside Distinguished Professor of Philosophy. His main research interests lie in free will, moral responsibility, and both metaphysical and ethical issues pertaining to life and death. The project conducted a Younger Scholars Workshop on the Riverside campus in May 2015.

But the possibility of the *soul's* immortality is seldom, if ever, considered. Yet, reasons for doing so seem obvious—even though a survey of a thousand people might never mention a single one. Why? Before reading this book, did you ever read or hear anything about either "immortality" or "souls"? If you attend church, synagogue, or mosque—even if just sporadically—you likely don't remember encountering either term—even though the word "soul" may have appeared in a hymn or a sacred reading. However, seldom would anyone expect to see or hear "soul" *and* "immortality" used *together* at any of those places.

A Hundred Years Ago

Yet, one hundred and twelve years ago, Reverend Henry Frank published a book worth acknowledging here. He was a New York clergyman as well as a philosopher and an author. In an Appendix to his book he wrote, "The prevailing conception of the psychic activity considers soul and body to be two distinct entities. The two entities can exist independently of each other. There is no intrinsic necessity for their union. The organized body is a mortal, material nature, chemically composed of living protoplasm and its compounds. The soul, on the other hand, is an immortal, immaterial being, a spiritual agent, whose mysterious activity is entirely incomprehensible to us. It is at the same time supernatural and transcendental, since it asserts the existence of forces that can exist and operate without a material basis. It rests on the assumption that outside of and beyond nature there is a 'spiritual' and immaterial world, of which we have no experience, and of which we can learn nothing by natural means."

Also, Ervin Laszlo's 2014 book with Anthony Peake, involves the existence of what continues to be known as the "deep dimension." Their book's title, *The Immortal Mind: Science and the Continuity of Consciousness Beyond the Brain*, makes a persuasive case for immortality of the soul. Laszlo wrote, "Although the Big Question has not been finally and definitely answered, nor will it ever be, we have good reason to believe that we are immortal." A footnote reads, "The book uses 'consciousness' and 'mind' interchangeably, while reserving 'soul' and 'spirit' to the spiritual and/or religious context." But Laszlo does *not* make this claim out of human desire. Rather, his book explains why immortality is his fervent belief!

A Personal Note

This book therefore explains why "immortality" is intrinsically involved with "souls." It also will try to make both concepts as humanly appealing as seems possible. But this will mightily depend upon your particular reasons for reading this book. These naturally can range from simple curiosity to a frank quest for the significance of human life and the hereafter.

Perhaps a brief commentary from the author about his background for this book might help. From my continuing personal search over a period of fifteen years, I now feel reassured about reunions in Heaven with my beloved wife of fifty-seven years. My earlier books described my experiences in personally caring for Betty at home during increasingly severe ailments. These included my growing frustration about inevitably losing her to death. For my first sixty-eight years, I was a Christian and a skeptic of everything paranormal. Yet, traditional religious dogma eventually became insufficient, as I found an increasing number and variety of reliable reports of experiential evidence supporting the actuality of God, Heaven, souls, and soul reunions in Heaven. Moreover, I have had an increasing number of experiences in which I "felt," often persistent, "suggestions" that proved to be very helpful. This strengthened my belief in my own soul.

Several years after beginning my quest, I decided to have a hypnotic regression through past life and into life-between-lives, like you read about earlier in the book. I drove to Detroit, Michigan while someone else stayed with Betty. There, I enlisted the help of Arthur E. Roffey, PhD *and* DD, a past vice president of the Society for Spiritual Regression. But I never could have expected what happened there!

The hypnotic induction process took me to my younger and younger memories, and eventually encouraged me to imagine times before my conscious memories, ending up in my mother's womb. I tried repeatedly but had to admit I could *not*. However, I did complain that I could hardly move my legs or arms—they felt like lead!

Roffey patiently assured me, "You *were* hypnotized!" He then explained, "A few people experience "blocks" which seem to be created because "the subject is *not* supposed to have access to those areas of knowledge," which I interpreted as "I was not supposed to go there!" I thanked him and drove back home to Betty. But I naturally felt stymied for a long time. I even considered repeating it later. Just what was it that I *wasn't supposed* to discover? However, I eventually made peace with myself, by accepting a mysterious decision that now seems wiser than me.

Still, I have the same difficulty that you might have with the idea of "eternity." Naturally, our entire lives were built around an acceptance that every living thing has a beginning and an ending. But the principle of eternity is "forever." So, rather than become encumbered with incomprehensible assumptions, you too may prefer to simply consider the Eternal Almighty as "being" (i.e., existing), just like everything else that you *can* perceive *now*. Just remember Elizabeth Kubler-Ross' promise:

> "Death is simply a shedding of the physical body like the butterfly shedding its cocoon. It is a transition to a higher state of consciousness where you continue to perceive, to understand, to laugh, and to be able to grow."

Martyrs and Saints

The Catholic Church has elevated many martyrs to sainthood after they lost their lives in defense of their faith. The Judeo-Christian Bible also contains the names of many martyrs who refused to deny their allegiance to God. Cathedrals may honor the revered with burial crypts beneath their floors and occasionally a visible stone monument or altar. But most religions realize that human bodies decay or, as the Catholic Church recently accepted, may be cremated. Immortality therefore consists of souls' survival of mortal death and their sojourn in Heaven between incarnations on Earth. As such, all souls are equal in God's eyes, neither hierarchy nor special rewards exist, and each soul willingly considers itself accountable for its host's intentions and behavior on Earth.

The Real You

The New Advent Catholic Encyclopedia has an extensive discussion of the concept and history of immortality. "With the birth of the Christian religion, the doctrine of immortality took up quite a new position in the world. It formed the foundation of the whole scheme of Christian faith. The following are the chief propositions involved in the building up of the doctrine:

- "The human soul is a substance or substantial principle,
- "It is simple or indivisible, and also is a spiritual being that is intrinsically independent of matter,
- "It is naturally incorruptible,
- "It cannot be annihilated by any creature,
- "God is bound to preserve the soul in possession of its conscious life, at least for some time after death, and
- "Finally, the evidence all leads to the conclusion that the future life is to continue forever."

Given the details suggested by experiential evidence up to this point in the book, you naturally might expect some suggestions about getting help from your soul. That is the subject of the next chapter.

Fifteen

Messages From Our Souls

*"We are not human beings having a spiritual experience.
We are spiritual beings having a human experience."*

Teilhard de Chardin
French Philosopher and Jesuit Priest

Teilhard de Chardin's message may still be shocking even after what you have read in this book. Of course, his perspective is that of a clergyman. Yet, you may not find many religious leaders today who will agree with him. However, I leave it to you to discern why.

But, as is suggested elsewhere in this book, his thoughts should never in any way seem threatening. Actually, they should seem reassuring, since this promises you survival and reunion in Heaven with your loved ones. Yet this is possible because you have a spiritual side as well as a human side, even though your human side remains the one with which you are obviously more familiar and more comfortable.

So perhaps the only way you may consider that you *actually* have a soul is *if* and *when* you "sense" it. Naturally, this is *not* by any of your five human senses: see, touch, hear, taste, or smell. Nor are you ever aware of your soul as part of your "waking consciousness." Rather, that "sense" likely will come as what is called "experiential evidence"—an unusual, unexpected, and subtle *feeling*. It may seem to suggest "where to look for something;" "what to do in an *uncertain* situation;" or even "don't!" in a *normal* situation—or something else like these. What it will be recommending is likely *not* what you normally would do!

One of these that I recently experienced is a good example. I was replacing a very small hearing-aid battery and it accidentally got caught on an angle rather than drop normally into its compartment. It seemed impossible to remove and correct, leaving me puzzled and frustrated. Soon I "felt" a "suggestion," very strange because it didn't make normal sense to me. "Open the drawer in the night stand and look at the back side of the battery compartment." There in the drawer was a package of round-headed brass paper fasteners (i.e., "brads"), each with two long thin, flat "nails" hanging down. The backside of the battery compartment had an open slit in the middle, perfect for inserting one of the "nails" to dislodge the battery! Eureka! I remembered buying the fasteners years ago but never knew where I had stored them!

This typically happens "out of the blue," just a feeling, perhaps like a suggestion or a restraint. But since you didn't know that you have a soul, you may have just accepted what you "felt" but dismissed it with little wonder.

For another example, I was driving on a two-lane road late one dark night. Both sides of the road were heavy with trees and shrubs. I had been talking with the passengers. Suddenly, thoughts about deer just popped into my mind. "What?" So I slowed the van. Twenty feet ahead, a couple of deer emerged from the overgrowth to cross the road. Others slowly followed, the last being a fawn—which I had to brake for!

Everyday Matters

Although much of this book has discussed our souls in a spiritual context, just remember that your soul consciousness *may be* the origin of your "waking" consciousness, as seems exemplified in Cicoria's out-of-body experience. So consider that your soul consciousness may have the same concerns that you have, although not able to remember its past lives or Heaven due to the "veil of forget-fulness." Yet it seems to retain its special soul capabilities that enable it to have a much different *perspective* from yours. In the two examples I gave, my soul consciousness seemed to "see" what I could not see and even "know" the future.

So remember Newton's earlier comment: "While soul memory may be hidden from the level of conscious awareness through amnesia [i.e., veil of for-getfulness], thought patterns of the soul influence the human brain to induce motivations for certain actions."

Yet, consciousness researcher Fred Alan Wolf cautioned, "Communication between soul [self] and [body] self is difficult at best. Often the soul [self] is not heard or becomes devastated in its attempts to reach the deeply embodied and preoccupied [body] self ... the language of the soul is not a language of logic and words, but instead is one that speaks through the heart and intu-ition, often most loudly when we are in deepest trouble."

Considerations

So there are aspects of everyone's lives that might be considered to enhance sensitivity and receptivity to soul influences and to encourage them:

- Be in the present moment, not worrying about yesterday or tomorrow.
- Trust your feelings. Be cautious of nagging or uncomfortable feelings.
- Think back to similar past situations. Try to take a neutral position now.
- Emotional needs, fears, desires, and expectations can interfere.
- Impulsivity is counterproductive.
- May be concerned with safety and welfare of you and your loved ones.
- Assistance in a decision or undertaking depends on its effect on others.
- Humility and gratitude for help seem to encourage it.

We likely analyze situations and rationalize the answers we want or could reasonably expect. But since soul messages seem to come "out of the blue," and maybe they arrive more often when we do *not* have "predetermined" answers.

So we might *first* become aware of soul messages because of the nature of their *content*. Remember, our souls have a perspective of both seen and unseen physical and non-physical reality—present and future—more than any information available to us. Possible examples include premonitions of a potential accident or danger; an alert for loved ones; or a suggestion for the location of a lost item or the solution to a problem.

Gut Feelings, Hunches, and Intuition

You may already have experienced something similar in what have been called "gut feelings," "hunches," or "intuition." Malcolm Gladwell's bestseller *Blink: The Power of Thinking Without Thinking* was based on the work of Professor Gerd Gigerenzer, director of the Max Planck Institute for Human Development in Berlin. Gladwell's book is filled with anecdotes in which someone's "gut feeling" proved true when confronted by false expert opinions.

More recently, Gigerenzer wrote his own book *Gut Feelings: The Intelligence of the Unconscious*. He uses the terms "gut feeling," "intuition," and "hunch" interchangeably and feels that these appear suddenly in our waking consciousness without an apparent source.

Perhaps one of the best examples of "following your gut" seems to have happened during Amateur Night at the Harlem Opera House many years ago. A skinny, awkward sixteen-year-old girl prepares to go fearfully on stage. She is announced to the crowd as a dancer. Then, moments before she appears, the announcer says she has decided to sing instead. Three encores and first prize later, Ella Fitzgerald was history.

Receptivity

Nancy Rosanoff's classic book *Intuition Workout: A Practical Guide to Discovering and Developing Your Inner Knowing* provides a series of exercises to make people more comfortable and effective in developing their intuition. She has conducted training classes for corporations, universities, and other groups for many years. Rosanoff stressed that intuition cannot be forced. However, we can learn to focus our concerns, questions, and decisions in such a way that they *invite* intuition.

One commonality among gut feelings, hunches, and intuition therefore seems to be the need to release ourselves from the typical constraints of our left cerebral hemisphere: logical, rational, and analytical. In other words, be able to *also* think—or even loosen up our concentration—in ways that invite gut feelings, hunches, intuition, *or soul messages*—whatever you call "it."

Morning Pages

Writing and periodically reviewing is a useful technique for all manner of purposes, including "felt" messages. Author Janet Conner tried a version called "morning pages" during her painful divorce. She said this "worked miracles." It seems she was prompted by a statement from Julia Cameron's book *The Artist's Way:* "Anyone who faithfully writes morning pages will be led to a connection with a source of wisdom within."

Conner's positive results led to her book *Writing Down Your Soul: How to Activate and Listen to the Extraordinary Voice Within.* Conner's Web site (www. janetconner.com) illustrates that she apparently struck a responsive chord with many people. She has published several books, conducts courses, and has a radio show called "The Soul-Directed Life." Ironically, the topic for one show was "The Call to Become Friends With Death."

Soul Messages

Each of us seems able to cultivate a relationship with our souls whereby we invite *and* honor soul messages in the intent in which they are offered—to help improve our lives on earth. It obviously is difficult to give examples of soul messages since they seem intended only for the host, the time, and the situation. As you might expect, however, there are principles for inviting and recognizing soul messages, including:

- Freely given, without demands.
- Patient and understanding.
- Offered in the spirit of empathy and compassion.
- Never for selfish purposes.
- Encouraged by acknowledgment and respect.

You read earlier that some of us adapt to whatever life hands us. Others may ask, as the world-renowned religions scholar Huston Smith did, "What is the meaning of existence? Why are there pain and death? Why, in the end, is life worth living? What does reality consist of and what is its object?"

So, in the next and final chapter, perhaps you would like to reflect about *your* life on earth in terms of the influences to which we *all* usually are exposed and how they can shape our lives. But in *no* situation should you judge yourself or others *unfairly* in hindsight.

Sixteen

The Never-Ending Play

*"Authenticity in our infancy
leaves us when we become self-conscious.
Forever after, we plan and behave
according to how we think others see us."*

Will B. Mee

The early Greeks called us actors on the stage of life and Shakespeare made it famous. We each seem to play a "role." Perhaps you have felt this way if you ever questioned the life you lead. Then, you might have briefly wondered if you were simply "going through the motions." Yet, this *is* the "reality" in which we each grew up.

You may be surprised by what child development professionals say about the different life stages we experience. This is not intended to remind you that anything was missing in your upbringing—our lives naturally vary considerably.

So probably the greatest value for you in this chapter is to reflect on your life at each of these stages—however far back you *can* remember—and consider if and how they influenced the "who" you now *believe* you are. Please do this privately to enable you to personally contemplate both favorable and unfavorable memories, assuming that there were some of both. In the context of such retrospect, however, you hopefully will *now* be able to view the past from a more mature perspective.

From Early Years

We subconsciously begin to develop our "role" from a very early age. Very few of us will remember the impact of early family influences before age three. We hopefully flourished on love and attention. To get that, for the most part, we behaved as we *thought* our parents wanted. Yet, we often got mixed messages and signals we weren't capable of getting clarified. So we frequently were reprimanded. That may have been the beginning of our *felt insecurity*. If recurring, this was imprinted in our "hidden memories," and may have continued to affect us for the rest of our lives.

"Felt insecurity" has many dimensions, but it is *not* what adults would probably call "being in danger." Consider that, from a baby's early viewpoint of his or her *new* world, everything revolves around him or her. Around two, however, he or she likely develops a sense of "self" (i.e., self-consciousness). But that new awareness could feel threatening, especially if the people and the events surrounding him or her don't *continue* to revolve around him or her. If recognized in this way, the "terrible two's" are better understood.

All too soon, however, we yearned for independence. We may have wanted to fulfill needs *not* already satisfied. Or simply to expand our knowledge about other people and things, retreating when necessary to the safety and support of our "home turf."

Consider too that each person is *unconsciously* molded by something that begins early in life. Clinical psychologist Louis Cozolino's 2006 book *The Neuroscience of Human Relationships: Attachment and the Developing Social Brain* explained how our *early* relationships with our birth mothers get us started. Remember too the crucial emphasis on "bonding" (i.e., attachment) and David Chamberlain's remarks facilitating this even *during pregnancy.*

Parents typically reprimand young children from the mother's or father's *logical* reasoning, but young children don't understand logic. Yet praise or encouragement for specific behavior *is* well understood, and a word or two of reassurance of *everlasting love* seems to work magic—especially following a criticism or reprimand. Remember, however, that consistently *mishandled* situations may have been imprinted in the child's implicit (i.e., subconscious) memory and may continue to affect him or her for the rest of his or her life.

Authenticity

As you looked back over your life, however, there was one very early period that is worth examining more closely. Remember that your right cerebral hemisphere was dominant in your life then, *before* your "waking consciousness," cognition, and ego developed. Perhaps this is why that time of your life has been called "authentic." This might best be described as being fresh, innocent, eager, loving, honest, and inquisitive—which resulted in caring and compassion, key traits of the soul—hopefully *before* you had any reason to question *felt* love and security.

Yet we never again will be as authentic as we were as young children. Although authenticity is a lost art to adults, some of its characteristics may have enabled early humankind to survive and develop with a sense of community. Moreover, consider that near-death personality conversions just might be a return to authenticity.

From Case Files

In John James's book *The Great Field: Soul at Play in a Conscious Universe*, he tells of a case from the files of the Massachusetts General Hospital, citing a well-known photo entitled "The Rescuing Hug." "Souls of twins," James wrote, "are known for their very close connections." The hospital staff felt that one twin would die. Each was in a separate incubator, as hospital policy required. Nurse Kasparian ignored orders and placed both in the same incubator.

Instantly the two snuggled together. The stronger one put her arm across her sister and held her close. The weaker one calmed her breathing to that of her sister's and both survived. James concluded, "Simply experiencing touch and sharing energies made her [the weaker twin] stronger."

Along the Way

Before long, other children came into our lives, possibly siblings and certainly playmates. We began trying to establish our own identity. If we had siblings, we may have been introduced to competition for parental love and attention. But it may have seemed that our behavior always was improper and our efforts never were enough. So we eventually found *artificial* ways to behave to get what we wanted. We literally began to wear "masks" suited to the situation. We became actors learning roles.

Things got more complicated when we mixed with peers and in-groups. Now we found ourselves paying close attention to the *image* of ourselves that we saw in "reflections" from others. Sometimes we had to sacrifice loyalties to parents and friends to gain acceptance from the in-group. Soon we had collected a variety of new behaviors and masks. Add this to any *felt* inadequacies about physical attractiveness, clothing, and possessions—and maybe even the family's standing, employment, or wealth. Compound this with risky behavior for attention and acceptance.

At times, some of us may have felt "left out" or flawed. For example, we often judge ourselves by the way *we believe* that others "see" us. Yet "others" can be cruel, especially if we succumb to their bullying or demands, while we yearn to be "accepted."

Parental influences never ceased, or so it seemed. Manners; school grades; home runs or touchdowns; best colleges, professions, and marriages; and so forth—the image *they* wanted us to portray. As we became parents, the cycle was repeated with *our* children. We wanted the best, for them *and* for ourselves. Not outright subterfuge, mind you, but just enough to keep up *our* façades. Sooner or later, the "performance" became the reality. We became the actors whose roles we developed and we lived.

You naturally believe that your current "self-image" is your "real" self. You likely spent long hours and hard work in reaching your goal. This is why it may be personally troubling *now* to even wonder whether you and your soul have conflicting beliefs, attitudes, goals, and the like. Yet differences may be insignificant unless they are extreme. Examples of dangerous contrasts have increasingly appeared on the world stage in roles of power hunger, greed, revenge, malevolence, and injustice.

From an early age, we learned to compete and to win. But sometimes we got mixed messages. Are we supposed to win at *any* cost? This may have introduced a belief similar to our primitive survival instinct. Yet, contrast that with the teachings of some very successful coaches in many fields, including sports, music, and other creative arts. They emphasize, "competing with *yourself*." In other words, developing your individual skills to the very *best* of your *potential*. Michael Newton's book for mental health professionals leaves us with a challenging claim: "During life we can become so distracted by the roles we play that we never learn who we really are."

Teenage Years

Developing and expressing independence begins early in life. By teen years, this reaches our insistence of controlling our own life. Naturally, parents consider this a challenge to their authority and wisdom. This may be compounded if the mother and father had *not* allowed the teen *some* freedom in decision-making earlier, in matters where *negative* consequences might have been experienced without harm. Only then might young people *realize* the potential results of risky decisions.

Remember that it will be the *third decade of life* before the human being "matures." The emotion-control and decision-making centers (i.e., prefrontal cortex) of our brains are not fully developed until we are in our mid- to late twenties. Therefore, for many years from early childhood on, satisfying the demands of significant others may become the driver in our lives. Unfortunately, we may need to continue searching for the reward we most need in order to flourish—love.

Love of self is *not* necessarily narcissistic (i.e., vain). But *self-respect and felt self-worth* are the keys to loving others. Remember, too, that *real* self-love (i.e., self-esteem) may have originated very early in life, depending upon how valuable *we felt* that our birth mother considered us to be! Then, throughout the first two to three years, our relationships with our birth mother and with significant others either reinforced or negated our very early impressions. But all of this was happening *without* our later awareness, with results that can last a lifetime.

Psychiatrist Elisabeth Kubler-Ross explained it this way, "[The] word 'if' has ruined and destroyed more lives than anything else on this planet earth [because] most of us have been raised as prostitutes—I will love you *'if'* ... From early years, this proviso is drilled into us: *good behavior and good grades can buy love.*"

Science and Academia

As we all grew up, many of us attended college and studied science. It seems only fair to include a natural influence *there* that may have shaped our beliefs about the material reality. This seems to have been best expressed by the late physicist Richard Feynman, the "father of nanotechnology." Feynman was a Nobel Laureate and the first individual to describe the precise science of manipulating matter at the molecular and atomic levels. He offered his views in his book *The Meaning of It All: Thoughts of a Citizen-Scientist.*

Richard Feynman, for all his achievements and recognition, was still a humble man. He stressed the need to respect uncertainty for what it is. He illustrated this with the gradual shift of attitude by a young college student from a religious family, as the student advanced in the study of science. Whether from sensing the enormity that science knows about everything, this student starts to question his or her religious background as studies encourage the "scientific method." Eventually, the student may have some doubts about God and God's involvement in our lives, maybe with encouragement from some of his or her professors. Their influence may result from academic opposition to the existence of any reality other than the "material." But remember that only faculty members and their peers are acutely aware of tenure refusals, censures, research grant and publication denials, and other efforts to stifle any scientific interest in the existence of anything *non*-material or spiritual.

Our Individuality

Each of us is unique just as our soul is. Even the basic template for our human development is subject to a variety of influences. Our lives are composites of differing experiences too, considering our thoughts, motivations, intentions, and reactions. Despite groups that we join, we want to be part of, or we are assigned to, we still retain our inner individuality. But each group may have admission requirements that demand partial or total commitments, such as beliefs, behavior, or contributions. These range from social niceties to terrorist martyrdom.

In everything today, our individuality is tested. We may seldom, if ever, be led to question how much we value our individuality. But the next section warns how technology has lured us into modern conveniences that discourage having "close friends." Very few young people realize the power and value of personal alliances, as Sherry Turkle illustrates next.

Alone Together

Imagine finding yourself in the middle of a crowd of young millennials and *everyone's* iPhone or Droid suddenly "dies." Unless you are over sixty-five, you know the pandemonium to expect. Electronic networking and the Internet have become their lifeblood. Many of them therefore aren't comfortable with having a face-to-face "conversation." They grew up without knowing the camaraderie and empowerment of close personal friendships.

MIT psychologist Sherry Turkle has assessed the outlook perfectly. Her book *Alone Together: We Expect More from Technology and Less from Each Other* is the most recent of three books she has written on the impact of electronic networking technology on society. Turkle paints a sobering and paradoxical portrait of human disconnectedness in the face of expanding virtual connections in cell-phones, intelligent machines, and Internet usage.

Furthermore, in his book *The Master and His Emissary: The Divided Brain and the Making of the Western World,* London psychiatrist and writer Ian McGilchrist warned, "With the advent of electronic platforms, we communicate in 'written' language *far more* than ever before." Our left cerebral hemisphere increasingly dominates our relationships with typically impersonal, often coded, and sometimes incomprehensible "text" messages.

Probably the most sinister impacts of new communication technology are the sometimes unintended sharing of risqué photos and the anonymous cyberbullying of others, neither of which likely would occur in face-to-face encounters.

Some experts have said that the effects of hyperconnectivity and the always-on lifestyles of young people will be mostly positive between now and 2020. *But* these experts also predict that this generation "will exhibit a thirst for instant gratification and quick fixes, a loss of patience, and a lack of deep-thinking ability due to what one authority referred to as 'fast-twitch wiring'"—left brain characteristics. A 2012 Pew Internet online article by Janna Anderson and Lee Rainie, "Millennials Will Benefit And Suffer Due to Their Hyperconnected Lives," captured this revelation.

Threats or Opportunities

As you read this chapter, chances are that certain times and experiences in your earlier life brought back certain "feelings" about people, situations, and events. Therefore it seems important for each of us to acknowledge—at least to ourselves—any attitudes we might have toward others or any circumstances that make us uncomfortable. This is a natural result of how we were reared—not that it was wrong, but it happened. Only as we acknowledge this can we rise above our *learned* personal limitations in our relationships with others today.

Now, children grow up in a world that is a radically different from the close-knit hamlet common in early America, which was often said to be the prime environment for rearing a child. We are bombarded with information from every conceivable source, demanding our attention. The sheer quantity of information we are expected to download in school grows at a virtually unmanageable pace. We are often asked to make split-second decisions, sometimes with limited information. Stereotypes of other people or cultures pervade our mental landscape. These stimulate subconscious responses programmed into us, without our having had any personal experience getting to know other people, groups, or cultures. Simultaneously, artificial role models are thrust before us, attracting our allegiance or our yearning.

Surrounding all of this is the startling upsurge in the extent of single-parent families. These individual parents, naturally committed to the nurture and physical and mental development of their children, must be commended for their tireless efforts to provide other necessities too. Equally or sometimes more important, are the legions of significant others who are responsible for the physical, mental, and educational development of our children through a dozen or more of the most critical years of their lives. Remember, we human beings do *not* reach maturity until our mid-twenties!

But I Can't Change!

Remember the earlier claim that the development of an infant's brain is *experience-dependent*? New pathways are developed and strengthened by experience—being *created and used*. Neuroscience has discovered that this can happen as long as we live! Fox example, Jeffrey Schwartz and Sharon Begley's book *The Mind and the Brain: Neuroplasticity and the Power of Mental Force* revealed the brain's ability to create new pathways *not* just in childhood but *also* throughout life! So consider the following recommendations by one who should know.

Kathleen Taylor, a professor at St. Mary's College of California, has a Web site named "NeuroTaylor." She reminds us, "Human brains don't just test beliefs against reality in labs. They do it whenever new stimuli challenge their ideas. If those [established] ideas are important, cherished notions, then the human response tends to 'adapt their beliefs to the world as they find it'. People defend their core beliefs as if they are part of their identity. They're dangerous things, strong beliefs, and they aren't usually given up lightly."

In a few words, continued brain development can require that you "bump up against people and ideas" that are different [such as] reading multiple viewpoints ... then reflecting on how what was learned has changed your view of the world. "But we need to move beyond that and *challenge* our perception of the world. If you always hang around with those you agree with and read things that agree with what you already know, you're not going to wrestle with your [previously] established brain connections."

The point here is to suggest a direction rather than an overnight goal. Perhaps start by taking a few steps toward becoming more "aware" of those around you. Realize that other people's "needs" range from their hidden feelings of insecurity, anxiety, or low self-worth to necessary provisions of food, clothing and shelter. Including others on your radar, so to speak, will help get your soul more involved in your free will choices and actions.

For Us All

Psychotherapist and researcher Michael Newton captured his beliefs in this way, during an interview by Tim Miejan:

> "I think what I have come to understand is that regardless of whether we are deeply religious in a traditional sense or have no religion at all, our immortal being transcends the human condition. In a sense, it transcends the human body. Our minds display the positive energy that governs who we are, and it also transcends time and space. For me, this shows a higher spiritual authority. One of the things I think that I have learned that has been very important in my own life is the great sense of order in the universe, that nothing happens by accident."

You still may be reluctant to initiate discussion with others on topics in this book. But we hope you will be informed enough to add your comments or to even offer your personal feelings in discussions that do arise. However, for humankind to realize that each person has a soul and to understand the implications that this holds for each of us and our loved ones, personal attention must rise above the present level of ignorance and disregard. It should not have to be necessary that each of us undergo an "actual death experience" to realize what the millions of NDE survivors have learned.

The Apostle Paul reminded us "When I became a man, I put away childish things" in 1 Corinthians 13:11. But just consider how grossly some of us have "put away childish things." Does the belief that death is "final" compel us to live life to its extremes? We may not only disregard the concerns and needs of others, but also refuse them the rights that *we* demand. Evidence of this abounds in our often-cruel world.

But have hope! Consensus is building! Ervin Laszlo, Stanislav Grof, and Peter Russell edited the book *The Consciousness Revolution* from excerpts of their two-day extensive discussion about the state of the world and its inhabitants. Imagine being able to listen in as three of the world's leading thinkers consider the paramount problems and potential solutions to what ails us all.

Another leading intuitive thinker, Ken Wilber, wrote a foreword to their book, in which he seemed to capture the essence of their challenge: It must *not* be the case of "we have to change others." Rather, each of us must play his or her part in "the same groundswell … to make more sense of our lives, and to lead happier, healthier, and more caring lives." Only as we all pull together can we achieve our dream. As we each play a part, no matter how seemingly insignificant, can all the pieces come together "leading to a breakthrough of spiritual awakening."

Christopher Bache's words in his book *Lifecycles: Reincarnation and the Web of Life* seem to capture the essence of human life with a soul perspective: "The sages tell us that to participate in this drama, we have only to 'pay attention.' Simply pay attention to what is going on right in front of us and choose wisely. At a time when we understood more than we understand now, at a time when we had the advantage of wise counsel, we chose this life. We can trust the benevolence of the Universe and be confident of our ultimate safety in it."

We've All Been There

Is there a message in what you have read in this chapter—other than recognizing the influences to which we *all* are exposed and how they can shape our lives? Yes! Consider that this chapter also applies to *every other person* you ever knew! The Native Americans used to recommend, "Walk a moon (i.e., month) in another person's moccasins to really get to know him or her." Unfortunately, many roles that we play discourage this.

This doesn't apply just to colleagues with whom you work or those in your neighborhood or leisure groups. It begins at home, with your spouse, your children, and other relatives. How well do you *really* know these individuals, especially if they are at a different stage in life than you are? Think back over the formative influences that you experienced, where the other person may *now* be.

This is the foundation of a concept called "empathy," truly reflected by the Native American saying. Souls try to help us live meaningful lives on earth. Our roles sometimes put us at a cross-purpose with another person, each of us with an agenda of "winning." Think about this the next time you disagree, perhaps sharply, with your son, daughter, or spouse.

Meet Your Soul

So I hope that you might be willing to try a few simple ways to let your soul know that you are aware of its presence. This may help you initiate a developing relationship with your soul. These acts may seem simplistic, but your sincerity will be evident and is the catalyst for magic results for others. The reason is that others may overlook how you behave or even forgive what you say, but they will *never* forget *how you made them feel!* This was paraphrased from Maya Angelou, the noted American author and poet.

- Sincerity is easiest to practice with your loved ones, whether caring, listening, complimenting, respecting, or agreeing.
- An argument requires two persons and is most easily prevented or reconciled if one is willing to honestly consider the other's viewpoint.
- Behind every person is a unique story yearning to be heard ... and often worth listening to.
- Each of us would love to have others understand us, but we must be willing to understand them too.
- Saying "Good Morning [or Afternoon]" even to a stranger costs us nothing but may help him or her feel "Somebody knows I exist!"

- Passing along compliments or assistance to other people, such as you have received, helps keep kindliness alive.

The words of British Prime Minister William Ewart Gladstone over a century ago help summarize this chapter: "*We look forward to the time when the power of love will replace the love of power. Then will our world know the blessings of peace.*"

An ancient Sufi story might complete this book on a light note. It involved three angels convening at the dawn of time to discuss where to bury the meaning of life, a secret so sacred that only the most worthy of initiates should be allowed access to it. "We should put it at the bottom of the ocean," one exclaimed. "No, on the highest peak," another argued. Eventually, the wisest angel spoke up: "There is one place no one will ever look. We can hide it in plain sight: in the center of the human heart."

I offer my very best wishes for you and for your loved ones. I trust that you will receive the contents of my book in that context, to simply share what I have learned.

Bibliography

American Museum of Natural History. "Black Smokers." http://www.amnh.org/learn/pd/earth/gallery_week6/rfl_index.html

Anderson, Janna and Lee Rainie. "Millennials Will Benefit And Suffer Due to Their Hyperconnected Lives" Pew Research Center, Washington, D.C. Feb. 29, 2012. http://pewinternet.org/Reports/2012/Hyperconnected-lives.aspx

Anthony, Sebastian. 2013. "Astronomers estimate 100 billion habitable Earth-like planets in the Milky Way, 50 sextillion in the universe." ExtremeTech. http://www.extremetech.com/extreme/152573-astronomers-estimate-100-billion-habitable-earth-like-planets-in-the-milky-way-50-sextillion-in-the-universe

Apocrypha, The. Internet Sacred Text Archive. http://www.sacred-texts.com/chr/apo/

Armstrong, Karen. *Visions of God*. New York, NY: Bantam Books, 1994.

Arnsten, Amy F. T. 2010. "Stress Signalling Pathways That Impair Prefrontal Cortex Structure and Function." NCBI. http://www.ncbi.nlm.nih.gov/pmc/articles/PMC2907136/

"Athanasius on Christ." Christian History Institute #108. https://www.christianhistoryinstitute.org/study/module/athanasius/

AWARE Study. 2009. http://www.mindbodysymposium.com/Human-Consciousness-Project/the-AWARE-study.html

Bache, Christopher M. *Lifecycles: Reincarnation and the Web of Life*. New York, NY: Paragon House, 1994.

Backman, Linda. *Bringing Your Soul to Light: Healing Through Past Lives and the Time Between.* Woodbury, MN: Llewellyn Publications, 2009.

Bain, Brian A. "Near Death Experiences and Gnostic Christianity: Parallels in Antiquity." *Journal of Near-Death Studies.* 17(3) Spring 1999.

Barclay, Rachel. 2014. "Stress and Trauma in Childhood Affect Gene Expression for Life." Healthline News. http://www.healthline.com/health-news/childhood-stress-affects-genes-for-life-072914#1

Bargh, John and Ezequiel Morsella. 2008. "The Unconscious Mind." *Perspectives on Psychological Science.* yale.edu/acmelab/articles/Bargh_Morsella_Unconscious_Mind.pdf

Beauregard, Mario and Denyse O'Leary. *The Spiritual Brain: A Neuroscientist's Case for the Existence of the Soul.* San Francisco, CA: HarperOne, 2007.

Beischel, Julie. 2014. "Assisted After-Death Communication: A Self-Prescribed Treatment for Grief." *Journal of Near-Death Studies* 32:3.

Berg, Yahuda. *God Does Not Create Miracles—You Do!* New York, NY: Kabbalah Publishing, 2005.

Bergland, Christopher. 2013. "The Size and Connectivity of the Amygdala Predicts Anxiety." Psychology Today. https://www.psychologytoday.com/blog/the-athletes-way/201311/the-size-and-connectivity-the-amygdala-predicts-anxiety

Blatty, William Peter. *Finding Peter: A True Story of the Hand of Providence and Evidence of Life After Death.* Washington, DC: Regnery Publishing, 2015.

Bowman, Carol. *Children's Past Lives: How Past Life Memories Affect Your Child.* New York, NY: Bantam Books, 1998.

Burkeman, Oliver. 2015. "Why can't the world's greatest minds solve the mystery of consciousness?" *the Guardian.* http://www.theguardian.com/science/2015/jan/21/-sp-why-cant-worlds-greatest-minds-solve-mystery-consciousness.

Bussanich, John. "Rebirth Eschatology in Plato and Plotinus," pp. 243-288, in *Philosophy and Salvation in Greek Religion,* ed. Vishwa Adluri, De Gruyter, 2013.

Callahan, Maggie and Patricia Kelley. *Final Gifts: Understanding the Special Awareness, Needs, and Communications of the Dying.* New York, NY: Bantam Dell, 2008.

Cameron, Julie. *The Artist's Way.* New York, NY: Putnam, 2002.

Catholic Encyclopedia. "Soul." www.catholic.org/encyclopedia/view.php?id=10963

Carroll, Roz. "An Interview with Allan Schore – 'the American Bowlby'." www.thinkbody.co.uk/papers/interview-with-allan-s.htm

Cayce, Edgar. Wikipedia. en.wikipedia.org/wiki/Edgar_Cayce

Chamberlain, David. *Babies Remember Birth: And Other Extraordinary Scientific Discoveries About the Mind and Personality of Your Newborn.* Los Angeles, CA: Jeremy P. Tarcher, 1988.

———. "The Significance of Birth Memories." *Birth Psychology* The Journal of Prenatal and Perinatal Psychology and Health 2:4.

———. "The Expanding Boundaries of Memory." *Birth Psychology* The Journal of Prenatal and Perinatal Psychology and Health 4:3.

———. "The Fetal Senses: Twelve, Not Five: A New Proposal." *Birth Psychology* The Journal of Prenatal and Perinatal Psychology and Health http://birth-psychology.com/free-article/fetal-senses-twelve-not-five-new-proposal

———. "The Sentient Prenate: What Every Parent Should Know." *Birth Psychology* Journal of Prenatal and Perinatal Psychology and Health 26:1.

———. 2012. "One Well-Hidden Secret of Good Parenting." http://dbchamberlainphd.com/2012/12/19/one-well-hidden-secret-of-good-parenting/

———. Chapter Ten "Prenatal and Perinatal Hypnotherapy." *Transpersonal Hypnosis: Gateway to Body, Mind, and Spirit.* New York, NY: CRC Press, 2000.

———. *Windows to the Womb: Revealing the Conscious Baby from Conception to Birth.* Berkeley, CA: North Atlantic Books, 2013.

Chamberlain David and Michael Mendizza. "Touch of Hope: Discovering the Mind of the Prenate." http://ttfuture.org/store/prenate_mind

Chamberlain, David and Suzanne Arms. Touch the Future. http://ttfuture.org/files/2/members/int_chamberlain.pdf

Cherry, Kendra. "What Is Attachment Theory? The Importance of Early Emotional Bonds." About Education. http://psychology.about.com/od/loveandattraction/a/attachment01.htm

———. "Cognitive Development in Early Childhood." An Overview of Early Childhood Development. About.com Psychology. http://psychology.about.com/od/developmentalpsychology/ss/early-childhood-development_3.htm

Chiron, C. et al. 1997. "The Right Brain Hemisphere is Dominant in Human Infants." NCBI. PubMed.gov. http://www.ncbi.nlm.nih.gov/pubmed/9217688

Chopra, Deepak. *How to Know God.* St. James, MO: Three Rivers, 2000

Christian History Institute. "#108: Athanasius on Christ." https://www.christianhistoryinstitute.org/study/module/athanasius/

"Christianity vs Islam." Diffen. http://www.diffen.com/difference/Christianity_vs_Islam

Cicoria, Anthony. "My Near-Death Experience: A Telephone Call From God." *Missouri Medicine.* 111:4:304. July/August 2014.

CNN. 2003. "Star Survey Reaches 70 Sextillion." http://articles.cnn.com/2003-07-22/tech/stars.survey_1_sextillion-big-number- universe?_s=PM:TECH

Conner, Janet. *Writing Down Your Soul: How to Activate and Listen to the Extraordinary Voice Within.* San Francisco, CA: Conari Press, 2009.

Cozolino, Louis. *The Neuroscience of Human Relationships: Attachment and the Developing Social Brain.* New York, NY: Norton, 2006.

Cranston, Sylvia. *Reincarnation: The Phoenix Fire Mystery.* Pasadena, CA: Theosophical University Press, 1998.

Cruse, C.F. *Eusebius' Ecclesiastical History: Complete and Unabridged.* Peabody, MA: Hendrickson Publishers, 1998.

David, H.P., Z. Dytrych, and V. Schuller. 1988. "Born Unwanted: Developmental Effects of Denied Abortion." Avicenum, Prague: Czechoslovak Medical Press.

Du Sautoy, Marcus. "Brain Scans Can Reveal Your Decisions 7 Seconds Before You 'Decide'." Exploring the Mind! http://exploringthemind.com/the-mind/brain-scans-can-reveal-your-decisions-7-seconds-before-you-decide

Feldmar, Andrew. "The Embryology of Consciousness: What is a Normal Pregnancy?" *The Psychosocial Aspects of Abortion*. Eds. D. Mall and W. Watts. Washington, DC: University Publications of America, 1979.

Fenwick, Peter and Elizabeth Fenwick. *Art of Dying*. New York, NY: Bloomsbury Academic, 2008.

Fenwick, Peter, Hiliary Lovelace, and Sue Brayne. "Comfort for the Dying: Five Year Retrospective and One Year Prospective Studies of End of Life Experiences." *Archives of Gerontology and Geriatrics*. 2010 Sep-Oct; 51(2); 173-9.

Fenwick, Peter. *The Hidden Door*. New York, NY: Berkley, 1999.

———. *The Truth in the Light*. Guildford, Surrey, United Kingdom: White Crow Books, 2012.

Feynman, Richard. *The Meaning of It All: Thoughts of a Citizen-Scientist*. New York, NY: Basic, 1998.

Fischer, John Martin. 2015. "The Science, Philosophy, and Theology of Immortality." University of California at Riverside. http://www.sptimmortalityproject.com

Forstadt, Leslie. 2011. "Children and Brain Development: What We Know About How Children Learn." http://umaine.edu/publications/4356e/

Frank, Henry. *The Scientific Demonstration of the Soul's Existence and Immortality.* New York, NY: The Alliance Publishing Company, 1903. (Harry Houdini Collection in Library of Congress)

Frankl, Viktor. *Man's Search for Meaning.* Boston, MA: Beacon Press, 1947.

Gephardt, Sue. *Why Love Matters: How Affection Shapes a Baby's Brain.* Oxford, UK: Routledge, 2014.

Gershom, Rabbi Yonassan and John Rossner. *Beyond the Ashes: Cases of Reincarnation from the Holocaust.* Virginia Beach, VA: A. R. E. Press, 1992.

Gershom, Rabbi Yonassan. *From Ashes to Healing: Mystical Encounters with the Holocaust.* Virginia Beach, VA: A. R. E. Press, 1996.

Ghasemiannejad, Alinaghi. "Iranian Shiite Muslim Near-Death Experiences: Features and After-Effects Including Dispositional Gratitude." *Journal of Near-Death Studies*: 33(1).

Gigerenzer, Gerd. *Gut Feelings: The Intelligence of the Unconscious.* New York, NY: Penguin Books, 2008.

Gladwell, Malcolm. *Blink: The Power of Thinking Without Thinking.* New York, NY: Back Bay Books, 2007

Gopnik, Alison. *The Philosophical Baby: What Children's Minds Tell Us About Truth, Love, and the Meaning of Life.* New York, NY: Picador, 2010.

Greaves, Helen. *Testimony of Light: An Extraordinary Message of Life After Death.* New York, NY: Tarcher, 2009.

Grille, Robin. *Parenting for a Peaceful World.* Gabriola Island, BC, Canada: New Society, 2014.

Guggenheim, Bill and Judy Guggenheim. *Hello from Heaven: a New Field of Research After-Death Communication Confirms That Life and Love Are Eternal.* New York, NY: Bantam Books, 1997.

Hart, Tobin. *The Secret Spiritual World of Children: The Breakthrough Discovery that Profoundly Alters Our Conventional View of Children's Mystical Experiences.* Novato, CA: New World Library, 2003.

Heineken, Christian Heinrich. AstroDatabank. http://www.astro.com/astro-databank/Heineken,_Christian_Heinrich

Hillman, James. *The Soul's Code: In Search of Character and Calling.* New York, NY: Random House, 1996.

Hunt, Valerie V. *Infinite Mind: Science of Human Vibrations of Consciousness.* Malibu, CA: Malibu Publishing Company, 1996.

IANDS. *Journal of Near-Death Studies.* International Association for Near-Death Studies. Durham, NC.

Immortality. New Advent Catholic Encyclopedia. http://www.newadvent.org/cathen/07687a.htm

James, John. *The Great Field: Soul at Play in a Conscious Universe.* Fulton, CA: Energy Psychology Press, 2007.

Jaynes, Julian. "Consciousness and the Voices of the Mind." McMaster-Bauer Symposium on Consciousness. *Canadian Psychology.* April, 1986, Vol. 27 (2). Reprinted in Marcel Kuijsten (ed.), *The Julian Jaynes Collection* (Henderson, NV: Julian Jaynes Society, 2012).

Jenson, Elizabeth. "The Argument Over Reincarnation In Early Christianity." Historia: the Alpha Rho Papers. epubs.utah.edu/index.php/historia/ article/download/578/448

Johnson, Sara, Robert Blum, and Jay Giedd. 2010. "Adolescent Maturity and the Brain." NCBI. http://www.ncbi.nlm.nih.gov/pmc/articles/ PMC2892678/

Kaplan, Rabbi Aryeh. 2004. "The Soul: Understanding the source of our soul and its eternal essence." Aish.com. http://www.aish.com/jl/sp/ bas/48942091.html

Kepler-22b. 2011. "NASA's Kepler Mission Confirms Its First Planet in Habitable Zone of Sun-like Star." http://www.nasa.gov/mission_ pages/ kepler/news/kepscicon-briefing.html

Koch, Christof. 2009. "When Does Consciousness Arise in Human Babies." *Scientific American*. http://www.scientificamerican.com/article. cfm?id=when-does-consciousness-arise

———. 2013. "A Neuroscientist's Radical Theory of How Networks Become Conscious." Wired. http://www.wired.com/2013/11/ christof-koch-panpsychism-consciousness/

Kramer, Miriam. 2015. "Jupiter's Moon Ganymede Has a Salty Ocean with More Water than Earth." Space.com. http://www.space.com/28807-jupi-ter-moon-ganymede-salty-ocean.html

Kubler-Ross, Elisabeth. "There Is No Death." San Diego, CA, 1977.

———. *on LIFE after DEATH*. Berkeley, CA: Ten Speed Press, 2008.

Lagercrantz, Hugo and Jean-Pierre Changeux. "The Emergence of Human Consciousness: From Fetal to Neonatal Life." IPRF. International Pediatric Research Foundation. http://www.nature.com/pr/journal/v65/n3/full/pr200950a.html.

Laszlo, Ervin, Stanislav Grof, and Peter Russell. *The Consciousness Revolution.* Las Vegas, NV: Elf Rock, 2003.

Laszlo, Ervin. *Science and the Akashic Field: An Integral Theory of Everything.* Rochester, VT: Inner Traditions, 2004.

Laszlo, Ervin and Anthony Peake. *The Immortal Mind: Science and the Continuity of Consciousness Beyond the Brain.* Rochester, VT: Inner Traditions, 2014.

Long, Jeffrey and Paul Perry. *Evidence of the Afterlife: The Science of Near-Death Experiences.* New York, NY: HarperOne, 2010.

Lorenz, Hendrik, "Ancient Theories of Soul", The Stanford Encyclopedia of Philosophy (Summer 2009 Edition), Edward N. Zalta (ed.) http://plato.stanford.edu/archives/sum2009/entries/ancient-soul

Lorie Peter. *Revelation: St. John the Divine's Prophecies for the Apocalypse and Beyond.* London, England: Labyrinth Publishing, 1994.

MacGregor, Geddes. *Reincarnation in Christianity: A New Vision of the Role of Rebirth in Christian Thought.* Wheaton, IL: Quest Books, 1978.

Mann, Charles C. "The Birth of Religion." *National Geographic* 219: 6.

Markham, Julie and William Greenough. 2006. "Experience-Driven Brain Plasticity: Beyond the Synapse." NCBI. http://www.ncbi.nlm.nih.gov/pmc/articles/PMC1550735/

McCarty, Wendy Anne. *Welcoming Consciousness: Supporting Babies' Wholeness From the Beginning of Life.* Santa Barbara, CA: Wondrous Beginnings, 2009.. http://www.scientificamerican.com/article.cfm?id=when-does-consciousness-arise

McGilchrist, Ian. *The Master and His Emissary: The Divided Brain and the Making of the Western World.* New Haven, CT: Yale University Press, 2012.

Mehta, D., et al. 2013. "Childhood Maltreatment Is Associated With Distinct Genomic and Epigenetic Profiles in Posttraumatic Stress Disorder." PubMed.gov. U.S. National Library of Medicine. http://www.ncbi.nlm.nih.gov/pubmed/23630272

Miller, Alice. *For Your Own Good: Hidden Cruelty in Child-Rearing and the Roots of Violence.* New York, NY: Farrar, Straus, and Giroux, 2002.

Monaghan, F.J. 1980. "Hypnosis in Criminal Investigation." National Criminal Justice Reference Service. www.ncjrs.gov/App/publications/Abstract.aspx?id=70940

Monti, Martin. "UCLA Psychologists Report New Insights on Human Brain, Consciousness." http://newsroom.ucla.edu/releases/ucla-psychologists-report-new-248299

Moody, Raymond and Paul Perry. *Glimpses of Eternity: Sharing a Loved One's Passage From This Life to the Next.* New York, NY: Guideposts, 2010

Moore, David. 2005. "Three in Four Americans Believe in the Paranormal." Gallup News Service. http://www.gallup.com/poll/16915/Three-Four-Americans-Believe-Paranormal.aspx?utm_source=position2&utm_medium=related&utm_campaign=tiles

Moore, Edward. "Origen of Alexandria." *Internet Encyclopedia of Philosophy* (2006). St. Elias School of Orthodox Philosophy. http://www.iep.utm.edu/o/origen.htm#SH3b.

Morse, Melvin. *Closer to the Light: Learning from the Near-Death Experiences of Children.* New York: Ivy Books, 1990.

———. *Transformed By the Light: The Powerful Effects of Near Death Experiences on People's Lives.* New York, NY: Villard Books, 1992.

———. *Parting Visions: Uses and Meanings of Pre-Death, Psychic, and Spiritual Experiences.* New York, NY: Villard Books, 1994.

———. *Where God Lives: The Science of the Paranormal and How Our Brains Are Linked to the Universe.* New York, NY: Cliff Street Books, 2000.

Myers, F. W. H. *Irreducible Mind: Toward a Psychology for the 21st Century.* New York, NY: Rowman & Littlefield, 2007.

Nagel, T. "What Is the Mind-Body Problem?" NCBI. PubMed.gov. National Institutes of Health. http://www.ncbi.nlm.nih.gov/pubmed/8319503

NASA. "NASA's Kepler Marks 1,000th Exoplanet Discovery, Uncovers More Small Worlds in Habitable Zones." January 6, 2015. http://www.nasa.gov/press/2015/january/nasa-s-kepler-marks-1000th-exoplanet-discovery-uncovers-more-small-worlds-in/#.VPtJGWTUvQo

New Advent Catholic Encyclopedia. "Immortality." http://www.newadvent.org/cathen/07687a.htm

Newton, Michael. *Journey of Souls: Case Studies of Life Between Lives.* St. Paul, MN: Llewellyn, 1994.

———. *Destiny of Souls: New Case Studies of Life Between Lives.* St. Paul, MN: Llewellyn, 2000.

———. *Life Between Lives: Hypnotherapy for Spiritual Regression.* St. Paul, MN: Llewellyn, 2004.

————. *Memories of the Afterlife: Life Between Lives Stories of Personal Transformation, With Case Studies by Members of the Newton Institute.* St. Paul, MN: Llewellyn, 2009.

New York Academy of Science. "The Emerging Science of Consciousness: Mind, Brain, and the Human Experience." www.nourfoundation.com/events/the-emerging-science-of-consciousness.html

Nour Foundation. 2015. "Beyond the Big Bang: Searching for Meaning in Contemporary Physics." http://www.nourfoundation.com/events/beyond-the-big-bang

Olson, James. *The Whole-Brain Path to Peace: The Role of the Left- and Right-Brain Dominance in the Polarization and Reunification of America.* Mineola, NY: Origin Press, 2011.

On Islam. 2015. "How Does the Prophet's Soul Return Back to Reply to Us?" http://www.onislam.net/english/ask-about-islam/faith-and-worship/islamic-creed/167078-the-return-of-the-soul.html

Osis, Karlis. "Deathbed Observations by Physicians and Nurses." *Parapsychological Monographs.* 3 (1961) Parapsychological Foundation.

Pagels, Elaine. *Beyond Belief: The Secret Gospel of Thomas.* New York, New York, Random House, 2003.

Parnia, Sam and Peter Fenwick. "Near Death Experiences in Cardiac Arrest: Visions of a Dying Brain or Visions of a New Science of Consciousness." *Resuscitation.* 2002 Jan: 52(1): 5-11.

Parnia, Sam. *Erasing Death: The Science That is Rewriting the Boundaries Between Life and Death.* New York, NY: Harper Collins, 2013.

Paul, Apostle. *Living Bible.* Wheaton, IL: Tyndale House, 1973.

Pelley, Scott. "Sixty Minutes." CBS. November 28, 2006.

Penfield, Wilder. *Mystery of the Mind: A Critical Study of Consciousness and the Human Brain.* Princeton, NJ: Princeton University Press, 1978.

Pike, James A. *The Other Side: An Account of My Experiences with Psychic Phenomena.* New York, NY: Doubleday, 1968.

Piper, Don. *Ninety Minutes in Heaven: A True Story of Death and Life.* Grand Rapids, MI: Revell, 2004.

Prescott, Gregg. "The Veil of Forgetfulness." In5d. http://in5d.com/ the-veil-of-forgetfulness/

Price, John W. *Revealing Heaven: The Eyewitness Accounts That Changed How a Pastor Thinks About the Afterlife.* New York, NY: HarperOne, 2013.

Price, Michael. "Search for Meaning." *Monitor on Psychology:* American Psychology Association November 2011. http://www.apa.org/ monitor/2011/11/meaning.aspx

Princeton University. "The Universal Consciousness and the Uniqueness of the Self." noosphere.princeton.edu/papers/.../bondies.universal.consciousness.doc

Ring, Kenneth and Sharon Cooper. *Mindsight: Near-Death and Out-of-Body Experiences in the Blind.* Palo Alto, CA: William James Center for Consciousness Studies, Institute of Transpersonal Psychology, 1999.

Ring, Kenneth. *Lessons from the Light: What We Can Learn from the Near-Death Experience.* Needham, MA: Moment Point Press, 2006.

Roberts, Paul. "Instant Gratification." *The American Scholar*, Autumn, 2014. https://theamericanscholar.org/instant-gratification/#.VXmSDVV3lBw

Rochet, Philippe. 2003. "Five levels of self-awareness as they unfold early in life."
Consciousness and Cognition 12 (2003) 717-731.
http://www.psychology.emory.edu/cognition/rochat/lab/fivelevels.pdf

Rodriguez, Constance. "The Subtle Energy Body: Your Passport to the Mystical Realms." *The Llewellyn Journal*. http://www.llewellyn.com/journal/article/1496

Romens, Sarah, Jennifer McDonald, John Svaren, and Seth Poliak. 2014. "Associations Between Early Life Stress and Gene Methylation in Children." Wiley Online Library. http://onlinelibrary.wiley.com/doi/10.1111/cdev.12270/abstract

Rosanoff, Nancy. *Intuition Workout: A Practical Guide to Discovering and Developing Your Inner Knowing*. Singapore, China: Asian Publishing, 1991.

Sabom, Michael. *Light and Death*. Grand Rapids, MI: Zondervan, 1998.

Schechter, Solomon and Kaufmann Kohler. "Didache or the Teaching of the Twelve." Jewish Encyclopedia. http://www.jewishencyclopedia.com/articles/5181-didache

Schore, Allan. 1997. "A Century After Freud's Project: Is a Rapprochement Between Psychoanalysis and Neurobiology at Hand?" *Journal of the American Psychoanalytical Association*. SAGE. http://apa.sagepub.com/cgi/content/abstract/45/3/807

————. "Effects of a Secure Attachment, Relationship on Right Brain Development, Affect Regulation, and Infant Mental Health." Infant Mental Health Journal, Vol. 22(1-2), 7-66 (2001).

————. 2007. "Psychoanalytic Research: Progress and Process—Developmental Affective Neuroscience and Clinical Practice." *Psychologist-Psychoanalyst.*

————. Chapter Twelve. "The Right Brain Implicit Self: A Central Mechanism of the Psychotherapy Change Process." *Knowing, Not-Knowing, and Sort-of-Knowing.* London, England: Karnac Books, 2010.

Schwartz, Jeffrey and Sharon Begley. *The Mind and the Brain: Neuroplasticity and the Power of Mental Force.* New York, NY: Regan Books, 2003.

Siegel, Daniel J. *Mindsight: The New Science of Personal Transformation.* New York, NY: Bantam, 2010.

Singer, Rabbi Tovia. "Does Judaism Believe in Original Sin?" Outreach Judaism. http://outreachjudaism.org/original-sin/

Smith, Huston. *Why Religion Matters: The Fate of the Human Spirit in an Age of Disbelief.* San Francisco, CA: HarperOne, 2009.

Soul. New Advent Catholic Encyclopedia. http://www.newadvent.org/cathen/14153a.htm

Spong, John Shelby. "God in the 21st Century." Speech at University of Oregon. http://www.youtube.com/watch?v=PwNmj5h1zds

————. "A New Christianity for a New World." September 3, 2015. Reprinted with permission from www.ProgressiveChristianity.org.

Stanton, Marcia. 2011. "How Early Experiences Impact Your Emotional and Physical Health as an Adult." This Emotional Life. http://www.pbs.org/

thisemotionallife/blogs/how-early-experiences-impact-your-emotional-and-physical-health-adult

Stapelfeldt, Karl, B. Stecklum, and A. Choudhary. 2015. "Hubble Sees a Young Star Take Center Stage." European Space Agency. http://www.nasa.gov/content/goddard/hubble-sees-a-young-star-take-center-stage/#.VQMSp2TUvQo

Steinhardt, Paul and Neil Turok. *Endless Universe: Beyond the Big Bang*. New York, NY: Doubleday, 2007.

Stepanek, Jeni. *Messenger: The Legacy of Mattie. J. T. Stepanek and Heartsongs*. Boston, MA: Dutton Adult, 2009.

Stevenson, Ian. *Unlearned Language: New Studies in Xenoglossy*, Charlottesville, VA: University of Virginia Press, 1984.

————. *Children Who Remember Previous Lives: A Question of Reincarnation*. Jefferson, NC: McFarland & Company, 2000.

Storm, Howard. *My Descent Into Death: A Second Chance at Life*. New York, NY: Doubleday, 2005.

Tart, Charles. *The End of Materialism: How Evidence of the Paranormal is Bringing Science and Spirit Together*. Oakland, CA: New Harbinger Publications, 2009.

Taylor, Kathleen. http://www.neurotaylor.com

"Teachings Concerning the Veil of Forgetfulness." http://emp.byui.edu/SATTERFIELDB/Quotes/Veil%20of%20Forgetfulness.htm

"Timeline of Christian History." Christianity In View. http://christianityinview.com/timeline.html

Torngren, Patricia. 2011. "Primal Parenting: Giving Babies the Best Start in Life." http://home.mweb.co.za/to/torngren/patparent.html

Trafton, Anne. 2010."Life Beyond our Universe." MIT News. http://web.mit.edu/newsoffice/2010/multiple-universes.html

Tucker, Jim. "Children's Reports of Past-Life Memories: A Review." *EXPLORE*: July/August 2008, Vol. 4, No. 4.
http://www.medicine.virginia.edu/clinical/departments/psychiatry/sections/cspp/dops/dr.-tuckers-publications/REI37.pdf

Turkle, Sherry. *Alone Together: We Expect More from Technology and Less from Each Other.* New York, NY: Basic Books, 2011.

UCSD. "Europa & Titan: Moons With Life?" http://earthguide.ucsd.edu/virtualmuseum/litu/10_3.shtml

van Lommel, Pim. *Consciousness Beyond Life: The Science of the Near-Death Experience.* San Francisco, CA: HarperOne, 2011.

Vergano, Dan. 2014. "Big Bang Discovery Opens Doors to the Multiverse." *National Geographic.* http://news.nationalgeographic.com/news/2014/03/140318-multiverse-inflation-big-bang-science-space/

Wade, Jenny. *Changes of Mind.* Albany, NY: State of New York University Press, 1996.

———. 1998. "Physically Transcendent Awareness: A Comparison of the Phenomenology of Consciousness Before Birth and After Death." *Journal of Near-Death Studies* 16:249-275.

Wambach, Helen. *Life Before Life.* New York, NY: Bantam Books, 1979.

Weiss, Brian. *Many Lives, Many Masters: The Story of a Prominent Psychiatrist, His Young Patient, and the Past-Life Therapy That Changed Both Their Lives.* New York, NY: Fireside Books, 1988.

————. *Through Time Into Healing.* New York, NY: Simon & Schuster, 1992.

————. *Only Love Is Real: A Story of Soulmates Reunited.* New York, NY: Warner, 1997.

————. *Messages From the Masters: Tapping Into the Power of Love.* New York, NY: Warner Books, 2000.

————. *Same Soul, Many Bodies: Discover the Healing Power of Future Lives Through Progression Therapy.* New York, NY: Free Press, 2004.

Westerlund, Marcel. 2007. "Healing With Advanced Hypnotherapy: A Science of Spirituality." https://www.rcpsych.ac.uk/PDF/Healing%20with%20Advanced%20Hypnotherapy%20-%20a%20science%20of%20spirituality%20Marcel%20Westerlund.pdf

Whitton, Joel, and Joe Fisher. *Life Between Life.* Garden City, NY: Doubleday, 1986.

————. *The Case for Reincarnation.* Potts Point, Australia: Somerfield House Books. 1998

Wolf, Fred Alan. "The Quantum Physical Communication Between the Self and the Soul." *Noetic Journal* Volume 2, No. 2, April, 1999.

51478035R00119

Made in the USA
Lexington, KY
25 April 2016